Gunsmoke and Mirrors

Gunsmoke and Mirrors

How Sinn Féin Dressed Up Defeat As Victory

Henry McDonald

Gill & Macmillan

Gill & Macmillan Ltd
Hume Avenue, Park West, Dublin 12
with associated companies throughout the world
www.gillmacmillan.ie

© Henry McDonald 2008
978 07171 4298 9

Index compiled by Helen Litton
Typography design by Make Communication
Print origination by TypeIT, Dublin
Printed and bound in Great Britain by MPG Books Ltd, Bodmin,
Cornwall

This book is typeset in 12 on 16 Minion.

5 4 3 2 1

Contents

Preface

This is nothing personal. Instead this is an assault on an idea that has taken hold in the latter years of the Irish peace process. It is an attack on a gathering calumny; namely that the Provisional IRA's thirty-year campaign of violence was somehow the logical and moral extension of the Northern Ireland Civil Rights Movement.

Throughout almost twenty years reporting on the Northern conflict and its aftermath, I have come across many individuals within the Provisional republican movement whom I have grown to like and in some cases even cared about. I have come to the conclusion that a large majority of them would never have become engaged in 'ordinary crime' or wanton acts of violence had it not been for the circumstances in which they grew up. Despite what the loyalists might think, I have also found the majority of them when operating on a professional basis to be entirely courteous, helpful and at times useful in the pursuit of stories. Moreover, their present ministers in government (a Northern Ireland government!) are among the most personally amenable and human in their handling of press and public. And I have realised that a number of them have themselves been personally damaged by the extraordinary events they have lived through. An even smaller number too from the hindsight of three decades are individuals tortured by the carnage and indeed the futility of it all, some of which they personally wrought upon others in their very own communities.

This is not about score settling. Rather it is to challenge an entirely fake orthodoxy taking hold even onto a generation that never experienced the horrors of the Northern Troubles: that the IRA's bombs and bullets expended during that period were done so in order that somehow Ulster Catholics could become equal citizens in the North of Ireland.

In reality 'Project Provo' was about the destruction of a state, i.e. Northern Ireland, rather than establishing equal citizenship within that very same political framework. For those that joined the Provo crusade the worst sin they constantly accused others from their own 'tribe' of was reformism. Advocating reform, in these crusaders' minds, was once tantamount to treachery and apostasy. The wild ones that signed up to this battle did not do so in order to run that state on any reformed basis.

This book is less to do with looking back in anger than securing a future based on clarity and truth. It is to set the record straight. To ensure that the 'struggle' just past is not re-written and twisted beyond recognition.

This is not to ignore the actions of other 'actors' in the tragedy played out roughly between 1969 and 1997. The violence of the loyalist terror groups was merely the vicious and logical conclusion of a twisted, bigoted unionist ideology cum theology that portrayed Ulster's Catholics as mere *untermenschen*. Indeed it was no accident that the first shots in the conflict were fired from loyalist guns in 1966 at a time when Unionist politicians, especially those on its religiously fundamentalist wing, were whipping up existential fears. At the same time the pre-Provo IRA was, by the mid-Sixties, not only re-grouping but moving away from its entire commitment to 'armed struggle'.

The Unionist politicians stirred up the killers and then walked away from them when the blood started flowing. The loyalist groupings themselves tended to indiscriminately attack the general Catholic population and cared little about distinguishing between their sworn foes in the IRA and the majority of their victims, who turned out to be politically uninvolved in armed republicanism. Both groups are almost equally responsible for the carnage inflicted on the Northern Catholic-nationalist community.

The British state too played its part in prolonging the agony. Their policies, stretching from ignoring the structural discrimination and gerrymandering until it was too late, through to the human rights abuses of Internment and the torture of suspects and far beyond to the use and abuse of killer-agents operating in both loyalist and republican organisations, all created the conditions in which a movement such as the Provisionals could thrive. Conversely, the role of sections of the Southern Irish nationalist establishment in fomenting the split in republicanism and providing justification for de-stabilising the 'failed political entity' (Charles J. Haughey's own words) post-1969 cannot be underestimated either.

This is not nor should it be a hostage to 'what-aboutery'. The crimes of others in the conflict are well documented and stand to be condemned throughout the world. Yet the armed insurrection that the founders of the Provisionals launched following the 1969 schism in the republican movement was meant for us, i.e. those of us on this island from a Catholic or nationalist tradition/background. This was 'our struggle' even if most of us never really wanted it. They carried it out on our behalf because they somehow knew better than we did. And yet now we are being asked to be grateful for all the wasted years and broken lives, as if the Ireland of today, at peace and enjoying unprecedented prosperity North and South, was somehow down to those who wreaked so much havoc in the name of the nation.

This is not to deride the achievements of those central to the peace process or begrudge their endeavours in bringing the violence to an end. But it is a reminder that the armed campaign was utterly unnecessary, unwanted, and even from the vantage point of the early Seventies, completely counter-productive. We should not confuse our gratitude to those who made ceasefires and compromises possible with our 'gratitude' to them for stopping the killing of Irish people in our name.

Overall, the purpose of this book is to expose the charade of gunsmoke and mirrors, to pull back the curtain at the side of the stage and reveal the true nature of the political outcome in Ireland today. It is a settlement that could have been realised and bedded down a very long time ago, well before one of the most futile mini-wars of the late twentieth century was ever started.

Henry McDonald
Belfast, 31 August 2008

Prologue
Return to Sender

At around 3 p.m. on Easter Monday 2007 there was a traffic jam at Pettigo, the County Donegal border village, just the briefest of strolls from Fermanagh over in Northern Ireland. The source of the disruption for drivers, many of them returning from their seasonal break in the county known to Northern Catholics for generations as 'God's country', was a gathering around a statue erected in memory of the Irish War of Independence. The monument is of a crouching IRA 'flying columnist' decked out in his long trench coat, Sam Browne belt and beret, rifle in hand pointing North towards the direction of the Fourth Green Field just across the virtually invisible frontier.

Beneath this volunteer set in stone was a small knot of republican bandsmen and women decked out in the ubiquitous black suits and berets, white shirts and black ties, the uniform of the republican band, all filed up in military fashion. They were looking up towards a clean-cut young man in a sharp suit reading aloud through a microphone, every bit the New Sinn Féiner — all scrubbed up and thoroughly de-militarised.

It was hard to make out exactly what the entire content of this Easter speech was, but in between the complaining klaxons from motorists, the radio blaring and children moaning, all desperate to get back home, it was possible to capture snippets of Pearse Doherty's address.

There was a reference to 'affordable social housing', and the party 'being in national government' — all pointers to the coming Irish General Election campaign, for which Sinn Féin had high hopes.

Doherty was regarded as a near racing certainty to capture a seat in Donegal South West, whilst overall some of the Provisionals' most optimistic supporters and sneaking regarders in the Southern Irish media (of which there are legion) even predicted the party would win between twelve and fifteen seats. Thus Sinn Féin would be an unavoidable partner for government, and Fianna Fáil would have no other choice but to go to Gerry Adams and ask him to join them in a new Irish coalition. In turn, this would put Sinn Féin into power both in Dublin and in Belfast. Once that goal was realised the party would then advance on two political fronts, synchronise legislative moves towards Irish unity and in the process scare the living daylights out of the unionists across the border.

The contrast, however, between Doherty, the epitome of the neo-Shinner, and the macho-militarism of the band brought in to play traditional republican tunes was jarring. The scene illuminated the two worlds the Provisionals were still trying to straddle in 2007. Doherty was exactly the type of candidate the Adams leadership was trying to sell to the electorate far beyond the traditional republican base: young, articulate, moderate-sounding, non-threatening, untainted by the burden or legacy of the 'armed struggle'. And yet here was Sinn Féin's great new hope in Donegal surrounded by lots of reminders of the Troubles just past.

This small ceremony also highlighted the contradiction between the past revolutionary rhetoric and the present Realpolitik the republican movement was now firmly committed to. Essentially Doherty's notion of 'national government' translated in political reality as junior partner in a Fianna Fáil dominated coalition, which was hardly in itself a revolutionary outcome after so many years of struggle and sacrifice.

In the Easter 2007 edition of *An Phoblacht/Republican News*, Doherty's speech had been flagged up alongside a number of set-piece events to mark the beginning of Sinn Féin's election campaign. Indeed the entire paper was peppered with advertisements for and references to party candidates all over the country. One ad, for example, was for a fund-raiser deliberately designed to resemble the ITV talent show *The X Factor*. Dubbed the *The SF Factor*, the ad included graphics with Broadway show lights introducing 'The Candidates'. This movie-cum-game-show style fund-raiser at Ballyfermot Civic Centre on Easter Saturday was also the curtain raiser for the party's Dublin campaign. Among the delights on offer for the meagre fee of €10 was Dublin South Central TD Aengus Ó Snodaigh, who for one night only would take the stage dressed up as Elvis Presley.

Republicans weren't just eager to do battle in arguably their most important electoral contest since the 1981 Fermanagh/South Tyrone 'hunger-strike' by-elections (which had propelled the party towards taking the ballot box seriously); clearly they were going to enjoy themselves on their way to power.

The Easter edition of *An Phoblacht/Republican News* was shot through with a growing sense of confidence, and to an extent cockiness, right down from the headline 'Preparing for government' across to the rather petulant epistle from Sinn Féin Tyrone Assembly man, the very amicable Barry McElduff. In a letter to the Taoiseach, he lectured Bertie Ahern on the anger of the Irish people 'for failing to share the wealth of the state'. McElduff also tellingly referred to the '26 Counties'; the word 'Republic' was not mentioned once despite the fact that it is the state the majority of the Southern population now owed allegiance to, the same state which was enjoying such unprecedented prosperity.

This attitude, however, exposed a weakness in the Sinn Féin flank South of the border. Most of the party's 'stars' were from the North, and many of them, particularly Gerry Adams, were eventually to alienate Southern voters by either failing to understand the dynamics of the Republic's economic success or simply by patronising that same electorate. Indeed his appearance on RTÉ's pre-election live 'Leaders' Debate' proved to be disastrous as Adams came unstuck when questioned on specifics as to how his party would steward the Celtic Tiger economy.

Easter 2007's *An Phoblacht/Republican News* also proved once again that the movement was still suffering from irony-deficiency. On page 5 there was a picture of a recent Sinn Féin protest at the gates of Leinster House. It had been called to demonstrate against the outgoing Fianna Fáil/Progressive Democrats' Corporate Manslaughter Bill. Sinn Féin TDs and party members were demonstrating because they believed the legislation lacked the power to put company bosses behind bars for preventable accidents in the workplace that killed or injured their workers. Arthur Morgan, the Sinn Féin TD for Louth and an ex-IRA member, held up a poster for the camera. It read: 'Employers have blood on their hands.'

Leaving aside the IRA's campaign during the Troubles and the blood shed by workers in the North caught in the crossfire during the 'armed struggle', in Dublin blood was still being spilt and some of those dying at the ends of gun barrels were the victims of the local IRA in the city.

Among those joining Arthur Morgan on the demonstration was Daithi Doolin, another new face of Sinn Féin, deemed to have an outside chance of snatching the last seat in Dublin South East, the constituency of their arch rival, the Irish Justice Minister, Michael McDowell. Doolin held up a placard asking: 'How many more must die?'

Two years before, a young Dublin man, Joseph Rafferty, fell foul of a Sinn Féin and IRA member in Doolin's constituency. The 28-year-old courier, who had one child, had a heated argument with a member of a Dublin south inner city family with strong connections to the Provisional IRA in the city. This row had stemmed from Rafferty spurning the sexual advances of the man's partner, who, in a fit of rage, spun an elaborate tale about how he had insulted her. The price Joe Rafferty paid for firstly rejecting the woman and then standing up to her partner was to be targeted by the Dublin IRA. In April 2005 Rafferty was shot dead as he attempted to start the engine of his van outside his apartment in Ongar, west Dublin.

Following the murder, the Rafferty family refused to be silent about the killing. They publicly accused the republican movement in Dublin of ordering the murder. Moreover, they denounced Sinn Féin for what they claimed was an outright lack of co-operation with the Gardaí investigating the murder.

So incensed were they about the attitude of Dublin republicans that Joe Rafferty's sister, Esther Uzell, announced she would stand in the Dublin South East constituency, her sole aim to highlight her brother's killing and to use the platform to challenge Daithi Doolin to denounce the killers and call for them to be handed over to the Garda Síochána.

The Rafferty family circle had to endure constant threats and intimidation during their campaign to bring Joseph's killers to justice. Esther Uzell had to move out of her home near Pearse Street to a different location in Dublin 2. Despite this she fought a high-profile campaign for justice and was even invited to the White House on St Patrick's Day 2007 where she was greeted by George W. Bush's administration.

Esther Uzell also received support and succour from the McCartney sisters. These east Belfast women had travelled the world to highlight the case of their brother Robert. He had clashed with members of the IRA two years earlier in a Belfast city centre pub. Beaten and stabbed by up to a dozen IRA activists from the city's Markets and Short Strand areas, McCartney died on a city centre street. The assault, which began inside Magennis's Bar on the night of the 32nd anniversary of Bloody Sunday, was followed by a forensic clean-up of the bar, the disposal of the murder weapon, a staged riot the next day to disrupt police searches in the Markets area and intimidation directed at anyone in the bar who might think of becoming an eyewitness for the police.

Both killings, one in Belfast, the other in Dublin, encapsulated a core problem for a movement trying to escape its recent past. On the one hand it was fielding a whole new slew of candidates across the Irish Republic, many of them with little or no history of involvement in active republicanism prior to the peace process. Yet the organisation also had within its ranks the rough and ready and once reliable cadres who had done the dirty work as well as the donkey work for both the IRA and Sinn Féin during the times of isolation and opprobrium. How could the leadership keep in check those who still believed they ruled the roost in the communities they came from, that they were the law, the power, the untouchables, while still attracting new voters and potential members from far beyond the republican base, especially in the increasingly middle-class Republic?

But as they marched confidently towards Election '07 it didn't occur to Sinn Féin strategists that the Republic was in reality another country compared to the North of Ireland. While Northern Catholics inhabited a morally inverted universe, in which a majority of them saw no problem casting their votes for a movement that had protected the killers of Robert McCartney, in the Republic the electorate saw things in a radically different way.

In this state the overwhelming majority still supported the Garda Síochána as well as holding the Irish Defence Forces in high esteem. Moreover they didn't take kindly to private armies exercising rough justice on the streets of their capital, especially when that 'justice' appeared to be nothing more than thinly veiled acts of petty revenge and communal intimidation. Nor did they care for being lectured to by Northern republicans about how they in the South should manage their own affairs, particularly when a majority in the Republic thought their 'affairs' were being handled quite successfully at present. As the election results would prove, the Southern Irish electorate, while extremely grateful to Gerry Adams, Martin McGuinness et al for bringing the Provisional IRA campaign of violence to a final, complete end, were also highly reluctant to allow these same Northerners to get their hands on the state levers of economic and social power.

Back on Easter Saturday night 2007 Aengus Ó Snodaigh, dressed as the Elvis of the Las Vegas comeback period, took to the stage. He chose to sing 'Return to Sender', a tale of spurned love told through a song about a love letter being sent back to its heartbroken owner over and over again. Ó Snodaigh's choice of Elvis song was to be both prophetic and apposite: the republican movement was transmitting a message to the Irish Republic, an enjoinder to the Southern voters to unite with them on their grand march towards a United Ireland, target date 2016, the 100th anniversary of the Easter Rising. Instead that electorate chose to 'return to sender', their rejection marking the defeat of a decade-long (arguably even longer) project to gain power politically in the two states of Ireland. 'Partition', as one commentator put it inside Dublin's RDS on the Saturday afternoon of that seminal election, 'still ruled OK'.

Chapter One
Casualties of War

The IRA's book of the dead was launched at a commemorative dinner dance at the City West Hotel in Saggart, Co. Dublin, on Saturday 13 April 2002. Admission was by ticket only and the guests included the relatives and loved ones of the 364 IRA volunteers and Sinn Féin activists who died during the Northern Troubles, each one memorialised in the pages of a hardback book titled *Tírghrá*.

Its publication in many ways signposted that the Provisionals' 'armed struggle' and the tactical use of arms was coming to a final end. Each individual copy of the book handed over to families, spouses or friends of the fallen was like that 'carriage clock moment', the handing over of the ubiquitous retirement memento marking the end of a loyal career spanning years, often decades, of service; a token of thanks for all of that and then good-bye!

Gerry Adams delivered the opening message on the night and his words are recorded in the first few pages of *Tírghrá*. Ever one to link the violence just ending to previous IRA campaigns of the twentieth century, Adams reminded the faithful that there were families in the audience that represented IRA members from the 1930s, 1940s and 1950s. However, the Sinn Féin President stressed that the bulk of those gathered in the west Dublin hotel that evening had ties of blood and marriage to those who died during the Troubles, roughly spanning the years from 1969 to 1997.

'Ireland's Patriot Dead [the English version of the title] is a remarkable "who's who" of our patriot dead from that period — the longest and continuing phase of the struggle for independence and unity of our country.'

Adams was right at least about that. The book was and is a remarkable series of pen portraits of those Provisional republicans who were either killed in the Troubles or died in accidents or natural causes during that time.

There are tributes to at least seventy volunteers who did not die as a direct result of the violence. They include many old pre-1969 veterans as well as a number of unusual characters such as the Aldershot bomber Noel Jenkinson, who defected from the Official IRA to the Provisionals while in prison for his part in the 1972 atrocity because of his opposition to the former's ceasefire that same year. A Protestant by birth and a convinced Maoist from the late 1960s, Jenkinson often visited Albania. One wonders what kind of Ireland this defector from the Officials dreamed would emerge out of the revolutionary seizures of the Provos' 'armed struggle'? Jenkinson died in mysterious circumstances while in prison in 1976, right at the height of the Maoist Khmer Rouge terror in Kampuchea, another movement he admired as a loyal 'Marxist-Leninist' opposed to 'Soviet Revisionism' abroad or the 'reformism' of his former comrades at home.

There are also several memorials to children, one as young as thirteen, who died on 'active service'. Members of the IRA youth wing 'na Fianna Éireann', some died as a result of British army and RUC actions, others died in 'own goals' (my quotes).

Of the remaining 294 who are remembered, many died as a result of accidental explosions or shooting themselves in bungled gun lectures or operations.

Even a cursory examination of the cold statistics in *Tírghrá* gives an insight into the true nature of the conflict. In fact the figures seriously call into question many of the myths the Provos erected around the 'armed struggle'; myths that continue to be propagated to another generation today. Because in the early years of the Troubles what is evident from the book of the Provo dead is that arguably the most lethal threat posed to volunteers came from either themselves or their own comrades.

The greatest carnage caused by 'own goals' occurred in 1972. In that most bloody year of the Troubles thirty-two IRA members died either while transporting bombs, constructing explosive devices or as a result of being shot, either by themselves or by one of their comrades. According to *Tírghrá*'s own figures, half of all IRA fatalities in 1972 were 'own goals'.

Overall the figures for IRA 'own goals' are instructive as to what kind of conflict the Northern Troubles quickly evolved into. Out of the 294 comrades to fall throughout the entire conflict, ninety-nine were as a result of their own bombs or guns killing them. In other words, around a third of the entire death toll for IRA volunteers were 'own goals'.

The bulk of these self-inflicted fatalities happened between 1972 and 1976. In that four-year period seventy-two

IRA members died in accidents involving their own bombs and guns. There were years, of course, when there were no such casualties at all. The death rate from 'own goals' tapered off between 1981 and 1983 when no one from within the organisation died in IRA 'accidents'. 'Own goals' none the less did continue to happen right up until the very end of the IRA's campaign. In its penultimate year, for example, starting from when the Provos blew up Canary Wharf in February 1996, the IRA suffered its last 'own goal' when Wexford-born Ed O'Brien blew himself up on a London bus whilst transporting a bomb. And although Ed O'Brien is commemorated as one of the last fallen in the 'struggle' within the pages of *Tírghrá*, it is worth noting that his parents forbade the trappings of a paramilitary funeral for him once their son's remains were brought back to Ireland.

Among the tributes to the 'own goal' dead is one for four young IRA men who died transporting a bomb in the east Belfast Catholic enclave, Short Strand, in 1972. One of the Provo fallen in that explosion was thirty-year-old volunteer Edward McDonnell. His personal pen portrait goes to show that the obituary-writers of *Tírghrá* were untouched by any sense of irony.

'He [McDonnell] had a great singing voice and a vast repertoire of songs but it was his rendition of Mary from Dungloe (his personal favourite), which, when called upon to sing at local functions or parties, brought the house down.'

By the time the Provos ended their violent and unsuccessful campaign to destroy the Northern Ireland state, they were regarded as among the most technically sophisticated terrorists/paramilitaries anywhere in the world. Their bomb-making expertise would be exported around the planet and used in places as diverse as Southern Lebanon, Colombia and latterly Iraq. In the case of Colombia the Provos would even be paid handsomely for their training and expertise, thanks to the narco-dollars of the ultra-left guerrilla army, FARC: the net product being the deaths of hundreds of civilians, many of them the poorest of the poor caught in FARC crossfire.

Yet the Provisionals arrived at this position as world leaders in the black arts of bomb-construction not only by learning but also by dying. Their learning curve, beginning with rudimentary timing devices such as condoms filled with acid (the crudest of incendiary devices used to set off fires in commercial targets), was littered with a trail of blood and gore, some their own, much more belonging to ordinary civilians and passers-by.

Moreover, for an 'undefeated army' which not only took on the might of British imperialism but also had to endure a sustained and supposedly Brit-directed murder campaign by loyalist proxies, the death toll in *Tírghrá* also raises some uncomfortable questions. Between their inception until the end of their armed campaign the Provisionals lost thirty-six volunteers to the various factions of loyalism; by contrast 266 more were killed in bungled operations involving bombs and guns. In fact, inside the official record of the PIRA dead as contained in *Tírghrá*, twenty-four volunteers are commemorated even though they were killed in road traffic accidents (the biggest consistent killer of them all during the Northern Ireland Troubles!). Less than twelve were deliberately targeted and killed by loyalist paramilitaries. Moreover, only 40 per cent of IRA casualties were a result of confrontations with their main enemy — the British army.

Many of these 'confrontations' were also not direct

military battles at all. In fact, the striking thing about the nature of the conflict was the extremely limited number of head-on clashes between IRA activists and British troops between the Provisionals' inception in late 1969/early 1970 and the end of the armed campaign three and a half decades later.

It became obvious by the mid-1970s that the 'armed struggle' that had so chronically de-stabilised Northern Ireland and pushed the North towards the precipice of sectarian civil war was settling down into a so-called 'Long War'. The Provisionals' strategists, particularly their Northern leadership, envisaged this struggle as a process of firstly vetoing any internal political settlement and in addition eventually sapping the will of the British government to shore up the Union, militarily, politically and financially. This latter goal would be achieved in large part by increasing the volume of body bags containing British soldiers being shipped back across the Irish Sea. As more English, Scottish and Welsh troops were sent home in coffins, the Provos calculated, the greater the pressure from British public opinion on their government to withdraw.

Even as late as 1989, fourteen years after Gerry Adams and co. devised the 'Long War' strategy, leading Sinn Féin and IRA figures still held onto the 'body bag' theory as the best way to deliver British disengagement. In an interview first published in the iconic soft porn magazine *Playboy* and later reprinted in March of that year by *Magill*, the Dublin current affairs magazine, Danny Morrison maintained that the republican movement's plan was still to sicken the will of the British with body bags.

'When it's politically costly for the British to remain in

Ireland, they'll go . . . it won't be triggered until a large number of British soldiers are killed and that's what's going to happen,' Morrison predicted.

Apart from high-profile UK political targets, the prime casualties of war for the Provisionals were clearly British troops. But if we take Morrison's prediction from the time-frame of his 1989 *Playboy* interview and the first IRA ceasefire in 1994, the Provisionals clearly failed in one of their key 'war' aims.

By the end of 1989 the Provos had re-intensified their violence, especially against the regular British army. Certainly, it had been a relatively bloody year for the British Armed Forces in Northern Ireland. The IRA had killed twenty-four British troops on top of those they had murdered among the locally recruited UDR and the police, the Royal Ulster Constabulary. Excluding 'own goals' and those members they shot as alleged informers, the IRA also killed six Catholic civilians and five Protestants totally uninvolved with loyalist paramilitary forces.

In 1990 marginally more Catholic and Protestant civilians died at the hands of the Provos than British troops, eleven to ten. A year later the gap widened with the IRA killing eleven civilians (again Protestants and Catholics together) compared to five British soldiers. By 1992 three British soldiers were killed in comparison to nineteen civilians; six Catholics and thirteen of Ulster Protestants and mainland British citizens combined. And in 1993, a year before the ceasefire, seventeen civilians lost their lives in IRA attacks and botched 'operations', eleven more than the number of dead British squaddies.

The majority of troops killed throughout the Troubles

were the victims of snipers, booby-trap bombs, land-mines and in some cases close-quarter assassinations, often when the soldiers were off-duty. It is worth noting that between 1969 and 1994 only ten republicans were killed in direct military confrontations with the British. Thus it is safe to conclude that the 'armed struggle' was not a classical guerrilla struggle where occasionally and often at key strategic moments in the conflict the rebel army would engage in open battle with their enemy. There was in fact no 'Tet' moment for the Provisional IRA, despite the fact that the Provos were so desperate to portray themselves as the Irish equivalent of the Viet Cong. So much so indeed that in the 1970s a republican support band wrote 'England's Vietnam', a ballad that compared the Northern Ireland situation to American woes in south-east Asia.

By 1989 the Provisionals were arguably the most well-armed and sophisticated paramilitary force in the Western world. Thanks to Colonel Gaddafi's largesse, PIRA had enough rifles to arm two infantry battalions, on top of the tonnes of Semtex and the large quantity of rocket launchers, the SAM missiles and flame throwers at their disposal. Yet despite the efforts of the likes of Jim Lynagh, the IRA's East Tyrone Brigade commander, the Provos never seized any 'liberated' territory. They did on occasion mount roadblocks in areas as far apart as Derry's Creggan estate down to the rural back roads of South Armagh. They were, however, unable to capture and hold onto for prolonged periods significant tracts of land during the Troubles. Their 'war' in reality was a campaign of assassination and sabotage or, as the former journalist and now world-renowned thriller-writer Gerald Seymour put it on Radio 4's *Today* programme in July 2007: the IRA's battle was a strategy of 'shoot and scoot'.

That is not to say there were no individual acts of battle-field-courage displayed by dedicated IRA activists prepared to lay their lives down. Indeed for hundreds who signed up they knew they faced a life where there was an ever-present threat of imprisonment, injury or death. Theirs was a frugal, mean existence. None the less they were unable to emulate the National Liberation Front of Vietnam or Algeria and create 'liberated zones', which those anti-colonial movements managed to turn into embryonic alternative states; in the Northern Ireland conflict, apart from a brief period before Operation Motorman and the creation of No-Go areas, this never happened.

By the end of the 1980s two conflict zones — one in the Middle East, the other in Northern Ireland — did at least bear some remarkable physical similarities to one another. At the time, I was living and working with Irish troops while researching a book about UN peacekeeping. Travelling across the edge of an occupied sliver of land stretching from the Mediterranean to the Golan Heights in Southern Lebanon, I could not help noticing the comparisons with South Armagh. On high ground in both areas, and in the Golan's case, on the summit of Mount Hermon, stood military fortifications that dominated the skyline. Once the IDF (Israeli Defence Forces) pulled out of most of Lebanon following its ill-fated 1982 invasion, the Israelis had constructed a network of heavily protected compounds, listening posts, helicopter pads and forward bases atop a ridge-line at the edge of their self-declared 'security zone', a buffer area between the actual Israeli border and the main

Shia Muslim population centres across the south. At the same time the British army had done something similar in South Armagh, seizing high ground across the frontier region onto which they built helicopter landing pads, look-out bases, mini-camps and spying facilities to monitor activity on the ground. The military building programme in South Armagh began in the mid-1980s when it became increasingly dangerous for military and police convoys to travel by road throughout what became known as 'Bandit Country'.

In both geo-strategical areas the compounds and the hilltop fortresses became frequent targets of their enemies on the ground. From the late 1980s until the Israeli army left Lebanon in 2002, firstly the pro-Syrian Amal and then the more intensely Islamist Hezbollah regularly attacked the bases, which were manned by the IDF 's puppet Christian-led militia, the 'South Lebanon Army' or SLA. At times the sorties on compounds, many of which overlooked villages and towns under the protection of Irish UN peacekeepers, were downright suicidal. Under cover of darkness Islamist fighters would infiltrate dead ground known as the 'wadi salouqki', a dried-up river valley running from just before the city of Tyre right into the Southern Lebanese hills where the compounds were based. Once the Amal or Hezbollah fighters set off 'Sagger' missiles or, at closer range, fired off rocket-propelled grenades, the wadis would be transformed into a free-fire zone. The attackers would be engulfed by mortar, heavy machine-gun and tank fire from the bases above whilst the valley below was bathed in light from the dozens of flares that the SLA or IDF shot into the night sky. Few of the fighters returned from these doomed missions, which were often seen by Irish UN troops both inside and beyond the 'security zone'. Indeed the fire fights became a ghoulish form of spectator sport for Irish blue berets stationed in the front line zone.

Eventually, however, thanks in large part to Iranian military supplies and training, the attacks on the compounds became less suicidal and more targeted. Heavy mortars and missile batteries were smuggled into the region and by the end of the 1990s, Hezbollah gunners were scoring direct hits on the compounds, many of these attacks witnessed again first hand by Irish UN peacekeeping troops. These increasingly sophisticated sorties, combined with an upsurge of well-coordinated attacks on IDF patrols both outside and inside the 'security zone', forced a re-think in the Israeli military establishment. Abandoning both their bases and their Christian allies in Southern Lebanon, the IDF pulled out under the orders of general-turned-Prime Minister Ehud Barak in 2002.

Britain's 'retreat' from South Armagh was a much less dramatic and far less hasty affair. Although police still had to be helicoptered into the region with military back-up, the British security forces never gave up their physical presence in South Armagh. In South Lebanon, on the other hand, beyond the mainly Christian (and thus at least nominally pro-Israeli) 'security zone', the IDF never maintained a long-term presence in the heartlands of their sworn enemies. There were no near permanent bases inside villages such as Brashit or towns like Tibnin, whereas the British, despite all the pressures and dangers, maintained a police station right in the middle of Crossmaglen. Unlike Hezbollah, the Provisional IRA failed to force the British army and RUC completely out of the 'capital' of Ireland's most rebellious territory. The British did not pull out under fire. 'Operation Banner' — the British government's involvement in Northern Ireland since 1969 — was to end during a well-planned, long-term programme of demilitarisation.

Ironically, the British army's pull-out to barracks only underlines the failure of the Provisionals' project. This is because one of the key enemies of their ideology was something so banal as normality. For while there were thousands of troops on the streets, many driven around in heavily armoured APCs and jeeps, the Provisionals could argue that the state of Northern Ireland was neither normal nor stable. The British military presence in effect was evidence of that thesis.

The republican military front in the conflict North of the border thus boiled down essentially to a campaign of sabotage and assassination. A breakdown of IRA 'operations' that ended in body count provides the evidence for this thesis, and exposes the myth that they were a conventional army.

Morrison's and Adams's strategy of generating 'war weariness' by sending the Brits back home in body bags was combined with the implementation of a cynical, often reckless and always bloody bombing campaign in Britain. According to this strategy, the twin-track approach of bringing the 'war' to the heart of the enemy, to hit Britain where it hurt, would eventually generate a 'Troops Out' movement akin to the anti-war sentiment in the United States during the late 1960s. A simplistic reading of the IRA's bombing campaign, especially the latter end of it when the Provos targeted high-profile institutions like the City of

London Stock Exchange, Heathrow Airport and even Number 10 Downing Street during the First Gulf War, was that it was all intended to break the will of the British establishment. While the IRA might have taken lives, caused tens, possibly hundreds, of millions of pounds worth of damage and massive infrastructural disruption, in reality their 'England campaign' never changed the dynamics of the conflict.

The idea took hold in certain London newsrooms in the early 1990s that the threat in particular to the City and the prospect of major global banks and finance corporations pulling out of the UK capital propelled the British establishment into negotiations with the IRA. What is illuminating now from the vantage point of post-ceasefire Northern Ireland is the contempt many ex-IRA activists have for this theory. Many of those who were deeply involved in the armed campaign (at least the ones prepared to speak frankly and who are not bound into Sinn Féin's mini-economies in places like west Belfast and Derry) are sceptical about the efficacy of the England campaign.

Here is what one former IRA volunteer told me about the thesis of the Brits being bombed to the negotiating table: 'The idea that we ended up in talks because of bombs in the City of London is utter rubbish. Let's get real here. The Brits pride themselves in being pigheaded. They didn't bend when the Luftwaffe was levelling British cities so they weren't going to bend to us.'

Another republican veteran, who like his comrade above asked to remain anonymous, drew a parallel with the current conflict in Iraq: 'It's no coincidence that the Brits are the only ones standing shoulder to shoulder with the Yanks in Iraq.

Truth be told — they [the Brits] can take it. It's almost in their DNA. They are under greater threat now in Southern Iraq than they faced against us in Ireland and they're still in places like Basra. Their presence might be doing more harm than good but they are there despite the dangers.'

These two sceptics are certainly not alone. Such sentiments are also repeated in one of the most underrated recent books on the IRA, written by the Spanish academic Rogelio Alonso. Indeed the most remarkable thing about Alonso's *IRA and Armed Struggle* is the refreshing honesty of his interviewees, the majority of whom were IRA veterans. One of them, for example, admits to Alonso that 'There was never going to be a military victory. The British government is nowhere near extended in terms of its commitment in respect of troops and armaments and security personnel to the Six Counties. It is probably one of the most sophisticated fighting governments in the world, so to even think that you were going to face down and defeat a British government was lunacy.'

Another of Alonso's interviewees also muses on the notion of British stubbornness. This IRA volunteer is sceptical about the efficacy of bombs such as the one that devastated Bishopsgate in the City of London in 1993: 'You are not going to bring the financial institutions of capitalism to their knees with one bomb. Hitler couldn't in the Second World War.'

Views like the ones above are peppered throughout Alonso's masterly study of the IRA's armed campaign and help debunk the myth of 'an undefeated army', let alone the supposed achievement of some sort of victory. No amount of 'spectaculars' in London or Manchester or even the 1984 attempt to kill Margaret Thatcher and her Cabinet in Brighton was going to alter the fundamental reality of the conflict, namely that it would only be solved internally via an historic compromise between the forces of nationalism, republicanism and unionism within Northern Ireland. Moreover, many of the bombings only produced a backlash against the Irish community in Britain, the overwhelming majority of whom were resolutely opposed to the IRA's campaign. It is worth remembering too that the British were able to foil many more attempts to bomb England throughout the Troubles than the ones the IRA successfully executed. In the 1980s many of these aborted or thwarted attacks were down to informers and agents back in Ireland. Sean O'Callaghan, the agent who exposed many bomb plots and saved the lives of Prince Charles and his then wife Princess Diana in the mid-Eighties, believes human intelligence was central to disrupting the IRA's 'England department' and thus helping to convince the Provos' leadership to end the conflict. O'Callaghan rose through the ranks to become Southern Commander of the IRA even while he was an agent of the state.

As in most civil conflicts it was civilians who bore the brunt of the Troubles. More than two thousand civilians, both Catholic and Protestant, lost their lives in the violence. A disproportionately high number of the civilian death toll was Catholic, around 1,252, more than 500 more than the number of Protestants killed. The majority of murdered Catholics died at the hands of various loyalist groups. Overall the IRA killed 1,781 people from 1970 to 2004, although that figure may be higher if a number of deaths, for example, connected to Dublin's gangland are also factored in. None the less the category of 'civilian' bore the greatest losses in that 34-year period. According to *Lost Lives*, the book which chronicles in forensic detail every single death of the Northern Ireland Troubles, a total of 644 civilians died at the hands of the IRA, some deliberately targeted; others caught in the crossfire or killed in IRA bombings.

Outsiders to Northern Ireland often point (with some justification) to the massive numbers killed in other civil wars or incipient civil wars of the late twentieth century such as Lebanon or Sri Lanka and point out that the North's population got off relatively lightly. In doing so they miss one crucial fact — the intimacy and geographical smallness of Northern Ireland. This has led to a legacy of tightly knit mini victim-communities based on blood ties and friendship. Moreover, beyond Belfast with its physical walls and barriers separating warring communities, in the smaller towns and villages across the North of Ireland, killers and victims have had to live side by side in relatively close proximity to one another. Given this nearness to the 'enemy' from either side, particularly to those that actually inflicted the pain, it is all the more remarkable from the vantage point of post-peace process Northern Ireland that this society has been able, relatively speaking, to move on.

It was inevitable in a 'war' fought out in built-up urban areas that civilians would comprise the majority of casualties. Yet even in the early years of their existence, when they were at their most casual and wanton, the Provos' leadership understood the negative political impact of civilian deaths. As far back as 1972, for instance — that terrible, bloody year — the PIRA leadership did their utmost to shield themselves from charges that they deliberately put non-combatants in the firing line.

In the early 1970s the Abercorn Bar at Belfast's Corn-market was a popular city centre bar frequented by younger people and off-duty British soldiers. In July 1972 it was the scene of a bombing made all the more gruesome by televised images of young women with horrific injuries being carried from the rubble. What started out as an 'operation' to murder British squaddies enjoying a Saturday afternoon's R&R ended in an early public relations disaster for the Provisionals. So, in order to counter the embarrassment and global opprobrium, the Provos deployed a fresh tactic that they would return to again and again and again: they simply lied.

One of the rising stars of the Provisional movement in the early 1970s was Ivor Malachy Bell, who rose through the ranks to become Belfast Brigade OC by the middle of the decade. In the book *Patriot Games*, in which his comrade Liam Hannaway linked the Provos' struggle back to the Plantation, Bell tried to shift the blame for the macabre scenes at the Abercorn elsewhere: 'My guess is that either the British army — the SAS — or some extreme right-wing unionist group is responsible for it.'

This, of course, was entirely fictitious. The Abercorn bombing had been executed by inexperienced young volunteers sent out by older, cynical men. It was akin to many of the disasters of the early Seventies where incompetence and a casual disregard for life were central factors. It was ironic too that Bell was using the same stratagem that extreme unionists had employed a year earlier following the massacre of Catholics at McGurk's Bar in Belfast's North Queen Street. Loyalists, led by the late John McKeague, put out a cover story that the explosion in the pub had been caused by an IRA unit who had gone for a drink to embolden themselves before they delivered the bomb. These, of course, were pure lies too. The UVF was behind the atrocity but they could not admit to it given the scale of the carnage and the loss of so much innocent life.

Throughout the Troubles, every time the Provisionals were responsible for civilian deaths, whether by accident or design, they resorted to the same old hackneyed excuses and worn-out mantras. Arguably one of the worst outrages occurred on Poppy Day 1987 when an IRA bomb exploded at Enniskillen's cenotaph and killed nine Protestant civilians. In the hours and days after the atrocity the Provos actually sought to put the blame on the British army for the explosion, claiming that British military surveillance equipment and communication frequencies had somehow set off the bomb.

Aside from the death toll and injuries inflicted on the civilian population, one of the most tragic consequences of launching the 'armed struggle' was the number of young lives that were blighted by joining up in the first place. The 'war' was, it could be argued, a 'children's crusade'. Many of those who died or went to jail for the PIRA in the early Seventies were barely out of their teens, some just out of their childhoods. By 1975, for example, up to 70 per cent of republicans who had gone through the Northern Ireland court system were under twenty-one years old. Furthermore, 63 per cent of those imprisoned were aged between seventeen and twenty-one. The 'war' was, in essence, an attempted youth coup, or to be more precise it was the fusion of the bitterness of old men with the burning anger of a new generation.

So if there was ever a defining song to accurately describe the first five years of the armed campaign it would not be some romantic nationalist ballad played on tin whistle and bodhrán, but rather an English pop song by glam-rockers Sweet — their anthematic 'Teenage Rampage'.

The motives among these young people for signing up to the 'struggle' certainly varied but two common factors emerge: a sense of grievance and thirst for revenge against the unionists and a growing hatred of the British army.

Even as early as November 1970, with the Provisionals still a fledgling force, there were clear signs of confusion in the minds of the fresh recruits to this very new type of IRA. The *Daily Mail*'s Leo Clancy visited Ardoyne, a Catholic enclave surrounded on three sides by loyalist strongholds in north Belfast and fast becoming a PIRA dominated redoubt in the city. The mood on these streets was one of overwhelming anger. One young rioter explained why the PIRA was gaining hegemony in Ardoyne: 'I hate the British, that's why I throw bricks at the army.'

Just seven days earlier, Clancy noted, the rioting had transmuted into terrorism when five British soldiers were injured in a nail bomb attack. The war was definitely now on.

In the course of his journey through Ardoyne's streets Clancy encountered an older man loyal to the Official IRA who explained why they had lost control of events on the streets. Meanwhile the teenage rioters Clancy came across gave some illuminating testimony as to why they were facing the British army: 'Who cares about unity with the Republic? You'd have to be crazy to want that. You get less on the dole for a start. . . . What we want is every peeler out of here so we can run our own affairs. I'll never be quiet until the army and the police stop trying to make us act like lapdogs for the unionists,' said Des, a sixteen-year-old apprentice electrician from Ardoyne during the 1970 riots in the area.

Another rioter called John admitted that he hated the RUC 'even more' than the British army. 'We'd kill those bastards,' John predicted, meaning local police. Within a short period of time they would be doing exactly that.

The reasons why so many young Northern nationalists signed up to the new army emerging from the streets of Belfast and Derry were complex and varied. Revenge seemed to be one of the dominant motives driving mainly young men into the arms of the Provisionals. The desire to hit back especially in Belfast, particularly at the 'Orangies', was overwhelming.

In the early 1970s Seamus Lynch was already an IRA veteran. Unlike his fellow dock worker Martin Meehan, Lynch had rejected the Provisionals and stayed loyal to Cathal Goulding and the Official IRA during the split. Lynch along with Meehan had been one of the republican movement's recruits back in 1966, the year of the 50th anniversary of the Easter Rising. Lynch recalled that just prior to the Troubles breaking out he was detailed by the Goulding leadership to start recruiting other fellow dockers in the city. A number of those from the New Lodge area they had asked to join recoiled in horror at the prospect. Yet within three years one of these men was now in the nascent Provisional IRA. Lynch recalled:

'It must have been around 1971 when I saw this man again on the New Lodge Road area where I used to live. There had been trouble between the area and the loyalist Tigers Bay along Duncairn Gardens. The local Provos had been getting ready to get stuck into the loyalists on the other side of the 'Gardens when the British army arrived in strength. We came up from the bottom of the road to observe what was happening. I noticed that the Provos were agitated at the presence of so many Brits between the New Lodge and Duncairn Gardens. Then I spotted the guy we had tried to recruit into the IRA back in the Sixties. He was raring to go and was disappointed that with so many British soldiers swamping the streets between the New Lodge and Tigers Bay he and his mates couldn't get attacking the Prods on the other side.'

One of the latter day reasons advanced by apologists for the IRA and Sinn Féin for the end of the armed campaign was the British state's practice of collusion with loyalist terror groups. The argument runs that the British armed forces, MI5 and RUC Special Branch ran the UVF, UDA, RHC and LVF as proxy gangs who would do the state's dirty work for them. The republican insurgency, according to this theory, was blunted and ground down by a conspiracy involving all wings of the security forces secretly directing loyalist assassins towards not just IRA activists but also Sinn Féin members and the wider nationalist community. State-structured collusion theorists also draw parallels here with South Africa in the latter years of Apartheid when the White Minority regime used the politico-paramilitary forces of the Zulus to wage war, often openly, sometimes clandestinely, on the African National Congress. Something similar, the authors of the Irish collusion theory argued, was going on in Northern Ireland, particularly towards the latter end of the Troubles.

However, if one examines coldly and objectively the casualties of war in the North of Ireland, the notion of a centrally directed, structured and state-run policy of collusion does not stand up to scrutiny. The evidence or lack of evidence lies in the graveyards of west Belfast, East Tyrone, South Armagh and Derry.

Between 1969 and 1994 the total number of militant republicans killed by loyalists was around thirty, which constitutes roughly 3 per cent of the entire victims of the UDA, UVF, RHC and LVF. In total the combined death toll at the hands of loyalists between the start of the Troubles and the first ceasefires was 1,005.

It is undoubtedly the case that there were individual instances of collusion where members of the security forces aided and abetted loyalist groups in targeting not only republicans but also nationalist political activists and even politically uninvolved Catholics. The case of the 1989 murder of Belfast solicitor Pat Finucane has become the most infamous and internationally renowned example of collusion. What has become apparent via the revelations both of police whistle-blowers like former RUC detective Jonty Brown, as well as loyalist informers such as the late Billy Stobie, is that two branches of the security forces not only knew the lawyer was about to be killed, but failed to prevent the assassination taking place. In addition it is now accepted that RUC Special Branch and the British Military Intelligence's 'Force Research Unit' had agents inside the UDA directly involved in the Finucane murder.

The ex-FRU British soldier known as 'Martin Ingrams', a former NCO, has revealed damning details of the role of army agent Brian Nelson inside the UDA and his role while working for the state in targeting Pat Finucane. However, Ingrams also revealed that 'collusion existed in all terrorist groups' and there were also British agents operating at high levels within the IRA. Two years before the Finucane murder Nelson was provided via his handlers with bogus intelligence that led to the death of west Belfast pensioner and veteran republican Victor Notarantonio.

The importance of the Notarantonio murder was related to whom the OAP actually died to protect. Prior to his death both the UVF and UDA had a top IRA man from west Belfast under surveillance from the vantage point of a flat on high ground in the Springmartin area of the city. From the apartment they were able to spy into nearby republican Springhill directly onto a house where the IRA activist was staying. When Brian Nelson, the informer, told his FRU handlers about whom his comrades in the west Belfast UDA were watching there was panic, according to Ingrams. Nelson was ordered to divert the UDA away from their target under surveillance. Instead the hit team were given intelligence documents based on Notarantonio's pre-Troubles involvement with the IRA.

Ingrams has since insisted he believes the original target of the plot was an agent of the British state within the IRA whom the FRU were extremely keen to see staying alive. In other words an old man long retired from active republicanism was sacrificed in order to protect a far more important asset inside the IRA of 1987.

The assassin in this murder was alleged to be Sam McCrory, an ex-Skinhead and close friend of Johnny 'Mad Dog' Adair. It was McCrory's first ever murder and propelled him up the ranks of the West Belfast UDA. He would eventually become officer commanding of the UDA prisoners in the Maze and he met Mo Mowlam in the months leading up to the Good Friday Agreement in 1998.

The ex-FRU soldier 'Martin Ingrams' has since met with the current PSNI Chief Constable and the former head of the Metropolitan Police Sir John Stevens and handed over information about both the Finucane and the Notarantonio killings. He is prepared to testify that officers in Special Branch and FRU were guilty of collusion in the Finucane case. But he is also adamant that collusion, when it occurred, was a far more complex phenomenon than one simply of brutal loyalist puppets killing on behalf of their British state masters. What's more, Nelson's career as UDA intelligence officer between 1986 and 1989 did not witness any large numbers of deaths among the IRA. Only one IRA volunteer died at the hands of the UDA in that period. He was Caoimhin MacBradaigh, who was killed at Milltown Cemetery by maverick UDA killer Michael Stone during his one-man gun and grenade attack on the funerals of the IRA trio killed by the SAS in Gibraltar.

'People have got to accept that collusion existed in all terrorist or paramilitary groups in conjunction with the forces of Her Majesty's government. It was not one-dimensional at all,' Ingrams insists.

More evidence for Ingrams's claim is found in the career of yet another high-placed state agent, this time inside the IRA, known by his codename 'Stake Knife', AKA Freddie Scappaticci.

The essence of the 'Stake Knife' scandal is that by the mid-1980s the British government was running an agent in the IRA who was himself in charge of catching informers within the Provos. Scappaticci was by then a feared individual both inside and out of the IRA. He was the Provos' 'spy catcher', the head of their internal security department, the unit tasked with smoking out police and army spies who had been recruited by the security forces. This man was not just a hunter of traitors in the IRA's ranks; unlike John Le Carré's fictional Soviet mole-hunter George Smiley, Scappaticci not only sought out informers and debriefed them, under often brutal forms of interrogation, but also personally executed them.

By the latter end of the 1980s 'Stake Knife' operated out of Dundalk, close to the border with Northern Ireland. During this time not only did he run the IRA's anti-informer unit but he was also an intelligence officer reporting to the Provos' General Headquarters Staff with a special role in running moles working for the republican movement inside both the Garda Síochána and the Irish army.

According to both Ingrams and the army agent 'Kevin Fulton', Scappaticci controlled at least one rogue Garda officer currently at the centre of allegations that he helped the IRA assassinate two top RUC officers in 1989. Canadian judge Peter Cory is currently investigating claims that the officer set up the double murder of Detective Inspector Robert Buchanan and Superintendent Harry Breen on 20 July 1989. The duo were ambushed on the main Dublin to Belfast road as they returned North after a high-level anti-terrorist conference at Dundalk's Garda station.

At the time of the double murder 'Stake Knife' was living in Dundalk and acting as the link man between the rogue Garda officer and the IRA's GHQ. Fulton has admitted that on at least one occasion before the Breen/Buchanan killing he drove Scappaticci to an isolated spot near the border for a clandestine meeting with the Garda officer.

Ingrams supports Fulton's view that 'Stake Knife' ran the agent: 'Scap was the officer's link man. He was the one taking the information off the Garda officer and passing it on in his role as an IRA intelligence officer to the GHQ,' the former FRU soldier says.

'The implications are explosive. Here was a British agent operating inside the IRA while living in another sovereign country, the Irish Republic. Here was a British agent corrupting and using police officers from another sovereign country to engage in crimes including murder.'

Ingrams's incredulity over this murky affair is compounded by the fact that, according to the IRA's original plan, the two RUC officers were meant to have been taken alive.

Central to the planning of the ambush was the IRA's then Chief of Staff based in Scotstown, Co. Monaghan, Kevin McKenna. According to senior figures in the Irish security establishment, McKenna's objective was to have the two RUC detectives abducted and then under torture interrogated. McKenna's prime goal was to extract information from them regarding the greatest single loss of IRA lives since the War of Independence: the SAS killing of seven East Tyrone Brigade activists at Loughgall the previous year.

The IRA's then Commanding Officers believed, rightly, that a mole from within the organisation, in all likelihood residing in the Republic, had passed on intelligence via the Garda Síochána to RUC Special Branch about the imminent attack on Loughgall police station. McKenna, a careful, suspicious man who trusted few outside his immediate circle, also believed that officers holding the rank of Breen and Buchanan may have had knowledge as to whom that informer may have been, or at the very least might hold clues to the informer's identity. Yet instead of being kidnapped and questioned by the IRA, the two RUC men were killed on the spot against McKenna's orders.

The Cory Inquiry into the Breen/Buchanan murders has yet to interview either Ingrams or Fulton. Ingrams says he is puzzled as to why Fulton has not been granted immunity from prosecution over any information he publicly gives to that inquiry. The ex-FRU soldier makes the point that Martin McGuinness was given full immunity for his testimony at the Bloody Sunday Tribunal during which the current Deputy First Minister of Northern Ireland admitted that at the time of the massacre he was the IRA's second-in-command in Derry. At the time of writing neither the Cory Inquiry nor the office of Northern Ireland's Police Ombudsman have questioned either of the former soldiers who played such key roles in the 'dirty war'.

Ingrams has his own theory as to why they have not been summoned thus far: 'I believe that the reason for this is that they want to gag Fulton, to make it more or less impossible to tell all that 'Scap' was up to at the time when he was living in Dundalk.'

Ironically, Scappaticci himself has sought legal representation over the Cory Inquiry into the Breen/Buchanan murders. 'Stake Knife' was in fact the first person to ask for legal aid in the event of him being called to face the inquiry in the Republic.

Whether he ever chooses to come forward and give evidence is extremely doubtful. The IRA mole hunter turned British agent has gone to extraordinary legal lengths to prevent reporters tracking him down or even writing about his current state of health. However, his role in the Breen/Buchanan affair sheds further light onto the true nature of the 'war' itself. Here, after all, was a key British agent operating inside the IRA, running its counter-intelligence department, who, according to Ingrams and several other ex-army and police officers, was killing and setting up for assassination dozens of people both inside and outside the republican movement. And it seems being allowed to do so with impunity.

On one level the 'Stake Knife' scandal is as serious as the Finucane killing in terms of a liberal democracy crossing the line between security and state-sponsored illegality and violence. On yet another level the revelation that someone so critical to the IRA's internal workings was an agent of the British state illuminates how much the Provos had been infiltrated at key strategic levels by the 1980s. Paradoxically, the 'Stake Knife' scandal raises yet another question mark over the claim that the policy of collusion using loyalists as proxy-assassins for the state was somehow centralised and structured. Given the depths of penetration the British security forces had reached into the IRA by then and thus the subsequent high-grade intelligence all its major security agencies had on the Provisionals, why then were there not far, far more republican casualties in the conflict? If only 3 per cent of loyalist killings in twenty-five years were IRA members (none of whom were either members of the Provisional Army Council, its GHQ or Northern Command), then what exactly were the British doing with such encyclopaedic information on the Provos?

What is becoming increasingly clear as more facts emerge

about the scale of infiltration is that if the British had wanted to, they could have used the loyalists to inflict massive physical casualties on the republican movement. One UVF member, at one time the organisation's second-in-command throughout Northern Ireland, confesses that among low level members of the security forces, most notably the part-time RUC and UDR, there was deep sympathy for the loyalists 'bumping off' active republicans. After all, many of these part-time local policemen and soldiers had seen friends and comrades killed by the IRA. He admits that photo-montages (the photographs, addresses, car registrations and personal details) of republican suspects were 'more common than beer mats' in the loyalist community. However, the UVF veteran is amused when he hears about allegations in the media of a widespread, centrally controlled collusion policy.

'If we had had a quarter or even less of the intelligence and aid our republican opponents said we had from the police or army, Gerry Adams would have had to spend every day walking behind the coffins of IRA men up the Falls Road.'

More skeletons in the guise of high-grade informers are falling out of the republican movement's lockers. Some of these may turn out to have occupied senior positions within the Provisionals. Indeed their old foes in RUC Special Branch, many of whom have retired from policing since the 1999 Patten reforms, have threatened to unlock many of these cupboards themselves. Some of these officers are angry that the focus on past crimes of the Troubles has been trained in a one-dimensional fashion: the role of the security forces in running agents inside the loyalist paramilitaries.

Undoubtedly the Provisionals tested their British enemies to the limit in the fields of security, intelligence and surveillance. If the prisons their foe put thousands of volunteers into became 'universities of terror', where inmates became equally educated and further politicised, then the entire theatre of operations of Northern Ireland also evolved into a giant laboratory for British counter-insurgency tactics. The Provos, it seems, weren't the only ones steadily climbing the learning curve during the Troubles; the British also learned a few things along the way.

Back in the summer of 1984 the new Provo leaders to have emerged from the North were bullish about the prospects of wearing down the British. In yet another strategically timed interview for *Magill* magazine, just a month before the Brighton bomb, Danny Morrison warned that despite recent electoral gains the 'war' would go on. 'And the one thing I have to emphasise, that all republicans are united on, is that electoral politics will not remove the British from Ireland. Only armed struggle will do that.'

He went on to say that he had 'absolutely no doubt that they [the IRA] will be successful in inflicting a political defeat on the British government'. Morrison did admit it was still going to be a long struggle: 'Yes, still in terms of five to ten years.' Ten years later there was a ceasefire and ten years after that key event, the Union flag was still flying over Belfast City Hall!

The notion then that the IRA ended on equal terms with their British enemy, that they were an 'undefeated army' who had fought their way into state power like ZANU and ZAPU PF did on their road to Lancaster House is a wholly false one. It is a myth that has taken hold retrospectively as some of those who started the 'war' seek current justification for all the carnage and destruction they wreaked. In doing so, they have at least achieved one unique thing — they have turned the Northern Ireland conflict just past into the first war ever in modern history where truth was the last casualty rather than the first.

Chapter Two
Everybody Went Surfing

It is the winter of 1975 and the stop/go, on/off ceasefire between the Provisional IRA and the British government is still in place, just. Only one anti-unionist political force has been consistently critical of the Provos' longest cessation so far, the Trotskyist People's Democracy.

From the day it was declared the previous Christmas until it was officially over in January 1971, the angry young militants of PD decried that the ceasefire was either a sell-out, an imperialist trap or indeed both.

In the January 1975 edition of PD's official organ *Unfree Citizen*, the party openly calls on the Provos to call off their negotiations with the British. 'We believe that many members and supporters of the Provisionals are alarmed and disturbed by the current negotiations,' the unnamed writer of the main article contends.

Fed up with the jibes and the barbs from their ultra-left flank, the Provos first attempt to ridicule PD. In its New Year edition of *An Phoblacht/Republican News* Sinn Féin denounces (with some justification it has to be said) PD as 'armchair revolutionaries' who had failed to fight the 'war' themselves.

PD then retaliates in its January 1975 edition of *Unfree Citizen*: 'We in PD are not in the habit of boasting about our courage but when the Loyalist onslaught comes we will not be found wanting in the defence of the minority.'

The party also personalise their assaults in print, singling out Sinn Féin's then Six County organiser Seamus Loughran for particular criticism. Loughran, a ruthless but tactically shrewd republican, then devises a cunning plan to undermine any sympathy for PD's uncompromising position within the rank and file of the Belfast IRA: he calls a mass meeting.

The Sinn Féin chairman invites a senior PD figure to address a large gathering of PIRA volunteers at a secret venue in west Belfast. There, the PD cadre is allowed to outline the party's critique of the ceasefire and their political analysis, notably that the North of Ireland is on the verge of a loyalist military coup d'etat. This was an unusual move for the ordinarily cautious, militaristic control freaks who founded and directed the Provisional movement's campaign. For Loughran it was a considerable risk given that there were many impressionable young men in the audience, some of the brighter ones immersing themselves in the 'Third World' struggle-fantasies of Franz Fanon's *Wretched of the Earth* or that bible cum guidebook of all would-be guerrilla/ revolutionaries anywhere, *The War of the Flea*. Loughran might have been concerned that some of the more leftist minded volunteers would have been seduced by the PDs' message. But the Sinn Féin chief in the North had an ace up his sleeve.

Following the PD activist's speech Loughran told the gathering that the Belfast Provos were in a dilemma. Their leadership was insistent that the ceasefire had to be adhered to, even though many volunteers opposed it. Instead Loughran saw a 'third way'. He asked the PD member how many cadres the party could mobilise in the city. If PD could provide a list of men and women then the Provos could provide each and every one of them with arms to continue to wage the 'armed struggle'.

According to some of those present, there was visible panic on the face of the PD representative. He started protesting that PD's role was not to prosecute the 'war' but rather to provide political advice, guidance and succour to the 'army' waging the real battles. In reality he had bottled out from the battle entirely. That lesson was not lost on those allowed to hear an outside voice deviating from the line of the PIRA leadership.

One PD member was later saved from the loyalists by the intervention of a journalist. He fled to Dublin after Jim Cusack, then of the *Irish Times*, discovered the existence of an Ulster Defence Association hit-list drawn up by its late leader John McMichael.

Cusack immediately contacted all those on the list including the PD militant who made the call to a return to arms back in 1975. The veteran journalist had saved the man's life. Meanwhile back in Belfast some of the young subjected to PD oratory and the call to arms were already back again waging the 'war'.

And it was a 'war' that was fuelled in part by the fantasies not only of the Irish ultra left but also their counterparts in Britain.

Thirty-two years later, in 2007, Nick Cohen published *What's Left? How Liberals Lost Their Way*, in which he attacks the self-deluding politics of many on the liberal left whose reflexive anti-Americanism and sentimental multi-cultural-ism has led them to offer support to pre-modern and anti-Enlightenment forces around the world. He condemns liberal reluctance to intervene against Serb ethnic cleansing in Bosnia in the 1990s, although it was happening on the borders of the European Union. Most obviously he excoriates the politics that allies first world liberals with reactionary forms of Islamic clericalism — movements and regimes implacably hostile to the post-Enlightenment secularism that is supposed to be the very bedrock of liberalism itself. He focuses strongly on those opposed to the US intervention in Iraq and on their motives. The book is challenging and uncomfortable — and it is meant to be. It is hard to recall any book of similar forensic power since George Orwell's *Homage to Catalonia* appeared in 1938.

Like Orwell, Cohen attacks the 'smelly little orthodoxies' of his own tribe in his own time — the British left. Orwell had risked his life in Spain and opprobrium at home for reporting truthfully and honestly the lies and crimes of sections of the left wing in Catalonia, specifically the way the Stalinist communists waged a war of annihilation against smaller Marxist parties like POUM even while they were all supposed to be struggling together against Franco's fascist forces. Now Cohen has also been demonised, not only in the UK but throughout the world's disparate left-wing community.

Cohen notes that those on the left who supported the so-called 'Insurgency' or 'Resistance' in Iraq were blind to the barbarism of these groups, due to the leftists' obsessive hatred of America. 'Imperialist' America and its 'lackey' or 'poodle' Britain has to be worse than even the organisations behind the suicide bombs and the sectarian assassinations in Iraq. The swp, the remnants of the old Workers Revolutionary Party, the various Stalinist factions and the Maoists also want the Taliban to win in Afghanistan because it will somehow herald defeat for us and British 'Imperialism'. Thus the Jihadists are somehow transformed into 'objectively' progressive. Even if the Trots and the Stalinists are repelled by the religiosity of the anti-Western terrorist movements waging war on the Americans and the British, the left somehow deducts that their triumph will undermine late capitalism and precipitate crisis and eventually revolutions across the planet.

This argument used to be called 'revolutionary defeatism'. Up until Adolf Hitler declared war on the Soviet Union it was the official policy of the British Communist Party to undermine Britain's struggle to repel invasion and defeat Nazi Germany. That was the first phase of 'revolutionary defeatism', a leftist fantasy shortcut towards the British revolution.

Revolutionary defeatism did not die with the Second World War. It remained part of the DNA of the far left, and some of it rubbed off on the mainstream left. Cohen offers detailed accounts of the bullying, control freakery of various far left factions, all deployed in the service of an apocalyptic end-of-days socialist vision — as mad and unforgiving in its way as the disguised religious cult it actually was. Among these micro-groups of the far left was the Revolutionary Communist Party (RCP). In between supporting the Serb genocide in Bosnia and defaming honest journalists from

ITN and *The Guardian* who exposed it, the RCP were once enthusiastic supporters of the Provisional IRA.

The RCP was not alone in this position, although it was more vocal than most groups of a similar kidney. It developed the Irish Freedom Movement, to help justify the IRA's 'war' with Britain. Throughout the Troubles the British far left clung to the bewildering illusion that a defeat for the UK state in Northern Ireland — in short a victory for the IRA and the achievement of a United Ireland on their terms — would in turn trigger the revolution across the Irish Sea! Apart from the fantasy involved in this analysis, it was deeply condescending. The Paddies were to be the cutting edge of a British revolutionary project; if this resulted (as it would) in sectarian chaos on the smaller island, wouldn't it be a worthwhile pawn sacrifice for the greater good on the 'mainland'?

Come the summer of 1994 and the first IRA ceasefire, however, these heroic revolutionaries are seriously peeved. What was this, that had the Islington hard left in such a paroxysm of outrage? The editorial in *Irish Freedom*, the organ of the Irish Freedom Movement, howled its anguish over the IRA's cessation of violence. 'Our job, therefore, is to expose and challenge the peace process for what it is — an act of continued British rule,' the RCPers fulminated.

Like the holy fools they were, the party had actually got something right for once: a unique moment of clarity. The peace process was all about an internal settlement within the existing borders of Northern Ireland. It was the only formula that had any chance of working. But the far left dreams in the RCP had at least spotted something real: if this was all that was on offer in the real world, what the hell had the last thirty years been all about? Yet another god had failed (see Arthur Koestler's account of his disillusionment with communism, *The Gods That Failed*).

There appears here to be a consistent psychological need stretching from support for the Provisionals all the way to cheering on the genocidal Serbian forces in Bosnia within this peculiar British leftist faction. The common denominator here has always been the wish to see their own country defeated and humiliated alongside a perverse sense of siding with one group simply for the sake of being contrary to a given consensus. Thus if the majority of the media and the political class opposed Serbian designs to ethnically cleanse Bosnian enclaves and break Muslim will in Sarajevo, in the RCP's bizarre mental universe true leftists should join the other side. However, this was and is not exclusive to such an eccentric and oddball British political faction as the RCP.

It wasn't just the far left fringe parties that became infatuated with the 'armed struggle' and its proponents and political apologists in Ireland. Some of those from the Marxist left who had shifted into the mainstream British Labour Party were determined to fuel the Provos' 'Troops Out' fantasies.

There had been many personal associations between IRA individuals and members of British far left groups over the years. For instance, Eamon Collins, whose memoir *Killing Rage* is one of the finest and most chilling books to emerge from the Troubles — it cost the author his life in exceptionally brutal circumstances — was patronised and backed by a lecturer at Queen's University Belfast who himself was an ardent fan of the Provisionals' armed campaign. As early as 1973 naive figures such as Labour MP James Wellbeloved (no doubt well-beloved among the Provos back in Belfast and Derry!) were drawing up petitions for immediate British withdrawal. There were petitions in the *New Statesman* from the mothers of some dead British soldiers and full-page ads from the great and the good of the liberal UK left calling for Troops Out regardless, of course, of the consequences. Into the 1980s — the decade when the left almost destroyed the British Labour Party for good — the likes of Tony Benn, Jeremy Corbyn and Ken Livingstone could be relied upon to keep up the simplistic Troops Out mantra.

No wonder that Gerry Adams and Martin McGuinness, at this time beginning to seize full control of Sinn Féin, were impressed. Or was it deluded? In an interview in the Dublin current affairs magazine, *Magill*, in July 1983, they concluded that 'there are indications now of changes taking place within the British political scene. The Young Liberals for example have come out in support of a policy of disengagement from Ireland and there are present discussions going on within the national executive of the Labour Party. There is also a lot of evidence a lot of British soldiers are fed up with what's going on in the North.'

You could hardly blame Adams and McGuinness for an analysis that in hindsight appears to be incredibly facile. The early Eighties certainly represented the peak period of leftist influence on Labour and led ultimately to the 1983 manifesto advocating among other things pulling out of Europe and scrapping Britain's independent nuclear deterrent. Besides that, this section of the British left had a long pedigree. Again we go back to Orwell; in his essay 'The Lion and the Unicorn', Orwell noted that:

> 'England is perhaps the only great country whose intellectuals are ashamed of their own nationality. In left-wing circles it is always felt that there is something slightly disgraceful in being an Englishman and that it is a duty to snigger at every English institution . . . the negative, fainéant outlook, which has been fashionable among English left-wingers, the sniggering of the intellectuals at patriotism and physical courage, the persistent effort to chip away English morale and spread a hedonistic what-do-I-get-out-of-it attitude to life, has done nothing but harm.'

The Provos were right about one thing, however. There was indeed 'an indication of changes taking place within the British political scene' in the early Eighties. Yet they were changes from which Sinn Féin could draw no comfort. Margaret Thatcher swept through institutional and corporate Britain like a right-wing hurricane. The Provisionals' leadership had simply backed the wrong horse, one that turned out to be a poor, spavined old nag that couldn't run a couple of furlongs. By the disastrous 1983 general election Benn and his allies were riding into obscurity. Livingstone, meanwhile, was still too marginal a figure on a national level — despite his ultimately becoming Lord Mayor of London — to influence government policy if and when Labour would ever come to power again. And yet the Provos continued to invest hope in the Bennite/Livingstone Troops Out fantasy, perhaps in the end for want of anything else to come along and deliver them Brits Out.

So when liberals and the sane left in Britain ask why someone like Livingstone can invite a radical Islamic cleric like Yusuf Al-Qaradawi to visit London in 2004, part of the answer lies in the traditional stance of assuming, always, that any enemy of the capitalist Tory is a friend. It is worth remembering that while Livingstone was paying visits to the Sinn Féin leaders on 26 February 1983, the other wing of the republican movement, the IRA, was bombing his home city. That is why he sees no contradiction in welcoming someone like Al-Qaradawi, whose views on gays (they have to die, it's just a matter of how to do it!), lesbians, Jews and women are so pre-modern as to be beyond satire.

The IRA 'pentiti' Sean O'Callaghan, former Southern Commander of the Provos, outlined to me how the leadership viewed Livingstone as a kind of British Marxist Messiah.

> 'The leadership was more enthusiastic about Livingstone than any other politician in Britain. Again you've got to remember that Ken had taken charge of the UK capital, that he was a national political figure and commanded huge support across the ranks of the Labour left. We were bombing London and planning more outrages across his city and yet here was its Mayor openly advocating our policy of "Brits Out" — why would they stop the war if they

could still count on support from quarters like that?'

Right up until the year communism collapsed, Red Ken was still offering instant solutions to the complex question of Northern Ireland. In his *Livingstone's Labour* published in 1989 he addresses the Irish Question again. Now in his chapter with the hackneyed title 'A Nation Once Again', Red Ken is putting years on the British disengagement plan.

'I believe that Britain should negotiate an immediate ceasefire with the IRA based on a guarantee of withdrawal in the lifetime of one parliament — no more than five years.'

He is literally putting years on his 'Troops Out' formula, from two years in *The Guardian* to five years in his manifesto for the 1990s. (It is worth noting that in the same book Livingstone predicts a rosy future for the USSR. In his chapter 'Third Revolution' Red Ken makes this prophecy: 'In 1917 Russia passed through its first two revolutions within the space of a single year. It then had to wait seventy years for the beginning of its third revolution. If that democratic revolution, which is now gathering pace inside the Soviet Union, succeeds, its lessons will be studied across the whole world and its impact will change the course of human history.' This is 1989, the year of the Tiananmen massacre, the Berlin Wall collapsing and communism crumbling across the planet; it is only two years before the USSR is dissolved and Russia itself re-embraces capitalism.)

Fortunately, there were some on the Labour left prepared to listen to the 'other Ireland' screened off by the gunsmoke and drowned out by the soundtrack of bombs going off. The most receptive faction turned out to be the Independent

Labour Party, once the political home of George Orwell. And here then another irony: the ILPers, who regarded themselves as the inheritors of the Orwellian tradition of democratic socialism, siding in particular with the WP, a party at the time regarded as almost as pro-Soviet as the Communist Party of Ireland. Truly in wartime common struggles can create strange bedfellows!

The ILP link is important because those cadres who were prepared to stand up against the pro-IRA left in Britain are today the same ones supporting democracy in Iraq and Afghanistan; men and women who are prepared to put aside their natural distrust of America and its foreign policies for the sake of the socialists, liberals and feminists whose only means of liberation, whether it be in Bosnia, Iraq or Afghanistan, was and is US intervention or support. From Ireland they have learnt a valuable lesson: just because a movement which is principally nationalist and by its actions at least latently sectarian wraps itself up in the trendy garb of 'anti-imperialism', that doesn't necessarily make it progressive.

The 'crime' therefore of a large section of the British and Irish left (with some important and honourable exceptions) was to not only abandon the genuinely progressive in Ireland North and South but also to feed the Provisionals' fantasies.

To be fair, there were honourable exceptions even among the Trotskyist fringe of British politics. As well as the democratic socialists of the ILP, the Militant Tendency had a much more realistic take on the 'armed struggle'.

Ted Grant, one of Militant's founders, in a 1994 pamphlet brought out in response to the IRA ceasefire, offered a blunt assessment of where the armed campaign had left the Provos: 'After a generation of revolutionary struggle, the PIRA has been forced to admit defeat. That is the long and the short of what happened.'

In *After the Ceasefire . . . Ireland, a Marxist Analysis*, Grant gets to the point immediately on page one. 'The declaration of an unconditional ceasefire by the IRA on the 31st of August 1994 represents a crushing defeat for the policy of individual terrorism . . . the IRA has declared a "complete cessation of violence" without having achieved a single one of its goals.'

Compared to the verbal and mental gymnastics performed by most British leftists vis a vis the IRA campaign and its ignominious end, Grant's analysis was refreshingly honest. In one section entitled 'A Blind Alley', Grant continues his blunt assessment of where the Provos have got to by the summer of 1994: 'Gerry Adams tries to put a brave face on it, claiming some sort of victory. But what has he gained?'

Grant is scathing about the revolutionary rhetoric of the Provisionals when compared to their Realpolitik. 'All the fine words about "revolutionary struggle" and even "socialism" (in the distant future when the border question is solved) finally boils down to this! John Major has given the IRA nothing. Nothing at least of any substance.'

Militant's founder also picks up the theme about the squalid futility of the 'armed struggle': 'Many who joined the Provisionals as fourteen- or sixteen-year olds are now middle aged and have spent all their lives fighting with no end in sight. Many are in gaol, serving long sentences. According to press reports, the republican prisoners in the Maze have declared in favour of the ceasefire.'

Unlike the British ultra-left cheerleaders of the IRA, at the very least Grant displays some true humanity in his writing even for the young men and women who signed up for a project as doomed and morally blind as the 'armed struggle'. This is to Grant's and the Militant Tendency's eternal credit. Other British left pamphleteers, however, played a much more malign role in distorting the complexities of the Irish Question and exalting the Provisionals' campaign to a pedestal it never deserved to be put on.

One of the most morally repugnant publications of the 1980s' British left was the *For Beginners* series book on Ireland. Aside from the simplistic take on the then present situation in the North of Ireland, the tone of this cartoon history veered from the sneering to the morally disgusting.

Take page 158, for instance, when the authors attempt to illuminate the murder of Earl Louis Mountbatten at Mullaghmore, Co. Sligo, on 27 August 1979. The cartoons include one of a British warship from the nineteenth century exploding. Mountbatten, Baroness Brabourne and two young boys actually died on a fishing boat yet the authors sought to use a naval vessel of war in their portrayal of the killing. Alongside the ship there are cartoons of Prince Charles alleging the murderers were 'bastards' (what an outrageous thing to say about men who planted a bomb knowing that an old man, an old woman and two young boys would be on board!) and the late Princess Margaret calling the Irish 'pigs' in the aftermath of the murder alongside a pig wearing a string of pearls. Below the cartoons is a balloon-quote from James Connolly, the words of which were not his own but rather those behind the comic strip: 'Margaret is wrong. [Presumably Princess Margaret.] The IRA bombs because it has been unable to develop any alternative strategy.'

In this section of the book there isn't a single reference to fourteen-year-old Nicholas Knatchbull (Mountbatten's grandson), 15-year-old Paul Maxwell or 83-year-old Baroness Brabourne, who, along with Lord Mountbatten, died in the explosion. Their absence from the book is a revolting, cynical editing of the facts concerning that atrocity; one which reduced the old lady and two children on board that doomed boat to the status of non-people. The absence of any reference to young Knatchbull and Maxwell and Baroness Brabourne is indicative of the immoral stance of a large section of the British left towards terrorism in Ireland during the Troubles.

(In a bitterly ironic twist to the Mullaghmore murders, Thomas McMahon, the cold-blooded killer who knew fine well that he was murdering two young boys and an old lady as well as a defenceless old man on that day, now likes to think of himself as a saviour of human life. He last came to prominence in the Irish media a year ago when he was arrested during a protest against the closure of a border hospital!)

The major ultra-left tendency to act as a intellectual prop for Provisionalism remained right up until the early 1990s People's Democracy. By then the party itself existed in name only. A group of activists such as Anne Speed, Sinn Féin's future candidate for the Euro elections in Dublin in 1989, decided to throw their lot in with Adams and co. while a smaller rump remained to keep the torch aflame outside of the Provo camp.

Adams himself, forever the consummate political chameleon, displayed an ambiguous attitude towards the PD 'vanguardists of the revolution'. While in Cage 11 at Long Kesh from 1973 to 1975, Adams recalled being deeply impressed by PD activist Michael Farrell's book, *The Orange State*, so much so that the future Sinn Féin President recommended it to his comrades in the prison. Moreover, Adams used Farrell's uncompromising dismissal of the entire unionist population as being as irreformable as the Afrikaaners as an intellectual weapon against the Official IRA and their new line of workers' unity and anti-sectarianism.

None the less Adams and the rest of the Army Council who came to dominate the Provo movement from the early 1980s onwards always had the measure of PD. Any drift into leftism within the Provisionals was viewed with suspicion and caution. An example of this occurred in the early 1990s at that year's Sinn Féin Ard Fheis, which was held in Dundalk due to the ban on the party holding their annual conference at Dublin's Mansion House. The previous year had seen a group of would-be left-wingers in Dublin force through a motion on the Sunday of the Ard Fheis committing the party to support abortion rights for women in the Irish Republic. This was at a time in the conference when most of the delegates, especially those from Northern Ireland or rural areas, were either heading home or in the pub.

Adams, according to several republican sources, was furious. Realising the dangers of alienating traditional Catholic nationalists, most of whom were fiercely anti-abortion (pro-life for the unborn while being pro-death when it came to the 'armed struggle'), Adams was determined to overturn the policy and he did so by calling on the loyalty of the IRA.

At the Dundalk conference the following year, IRA activists hand-picked by the Commanding Officers of Active Service Units across the North of Ireland were under orders to wipe the pro-abortion policy off the party's manifesto. Observers at the conference noticed swathes of young men in leather jackets voting in unison at the nod of a head from their OCs as Adams moved Sinn Féin back from pro-choice to no policy at all on the abortion question. Here was a classic case where the rhetoric of revolutionary leftism clashed with the pragmatism of populist Catholic nationalism. And there was, of course, only ever going to be one winner.

By the late 1980s the Irish ultra left had become withered by the ravages of time and the disappointment that the revolution was not going to happen in their lifetime. Many yearned for the 'Good Old Days' of their youth when the prospect of rebellion and the seizure of power seemed somehow real. Many also sought refuge in Arcadian recollection.

In 1988 Brandon Press published a series of recollections, entitled *Twenty Years On*, on the meaning for Ireland of the revolutionary convulsions of 1968, edited by veteran PDer Michael Farrell. There were contributions from, among others, Gerry Adams, who in an early example of twisting history (something he was to make an art form out of in the post-ceasefire world), the Sinn Féin President tried to link the reformist demands of the peaceful Northern Ireland Civil Rights Movement to the Provos' armed campaign. The contributors also included several ex-PD veterans such as '68 student activist and feminist Margaret Ward. Her chapter 'From Civil Rights to Women's Rights' was and is illuminating in terms of the illusions of the ultra-left and their disconnection from political reality, especially from that of the real-life working class.

An example of this was her Arcadian musing on a PD-organised festival in June 1969 inside the grounds of Belfast Castle, a gathering of the dreamers who were about to unknowingly sleepwalk into a sectarian nightmare two months later. Ward paints a bucolic picture of what life might be like under a PD-inspired Trotskyist Workers Republic.

'It was the first time I had seen children at a political event and the first time I had seen the children of Peoples Democracy members, such was the split between the personal and the political. As people sat strumming guitars and children played in the grass I had, for the first time, an awareness of what a future socialist society could be like.'

Around the same time as this twenty-years-on-nostalgia-fest went on sale, the American satirist P. J. O'Rourke was touring around the capitals of Eastern Europe, in the Stalinist 'People's Democracies' of the Warsaw Pact. O'Rourke concluded that the most notable thing about life under communism was not so much the ideological threat these societies posed to the West or indeed the various privations and sacrifices the workers had to make in the name of the 'workers' state'. The overpowering theme of these states, O'Rourke wryly noted, was how mind-numbingly boring life was for everyone trapped inside them. The same could be said for the vision of all of the PD-happy campers acting out their revolutionary fantasies underneath the shadow of Belfast Castle: a dreary, self-righteous, humourless organised fun camp, a boring Butlins-for-Leninists.

The trouble, of course, with this type of utopianism was that it was never going to be somehow reached through the wave of armed insurrection in the North of Ireland. The comrades of the vanguard were to be gravely disappointed.

The British and Irish leftists who gave what they called critical support to the doomed campaign have today divided roughly into two camps. One now depicts the peace process as a sham or a sell-out; the other rewrites history and portrays its engagement with the IRA and Sinn Féin — even while bombs were still killing British and Irish workers — as the first fledgling steps in aiding the Provisionals towards embracing purely peaceful politics. Some have even tried to take some credit for the later political machinations of Adams and his allies. This latter group has adopted classic Orwellian language and logic, once more turning war into peace. As late as May 2003, for instance, we see Labour left-wing MP John McDonnell claiming the Provisionals' campaign of sabotage and assassination was in reality a project for lasting peace. In an interview with Nick Watt, *The Guardian*'s Political Correspondent, on 31 May, McDonnell claimed:

> 'It's about time we started honouring those people involved in the armed struggle. It was the bombs and bullets and sacrifice made by the likes of Bobby Sands that brought Britain to the negotiating table. The peace process we now have is due to having to face some hard and painful truths including this one: "Without the armed struggle of the IRA over the last 30 years, the Good Friday Agreement would not have acknowledged the legitimacy of the aspirations of the Irish people for a united Ireland." And without that acknowledgement we would have no peace process.'

These remarks are surely in contention for the award for the most idiotic utterance ever made by a politician anywhere in relation to Northern Ireland's Troubles. Its overall 'logic' is gloriously Orwellian in nature, where the pursuit of 'war' was in fact the secret struggle for peace. Therefore in McDonnell's bizarre mental universe the IRA set out to murder and maim, risking the lives of tens of thousands of civilians as well as their own members, to reach a settlement which recognised the reality of partition and the principle of unionist consent, i.e. the Good Friday Agreement and latterly the 2006 deal at St Andrews. After this arrant nonsense from a politician who tried unsuccessfully to lead the British Labour Party post-Tony Blair, there is surely nothing else left to be said about the role the far left allies of the Provisionals played in prolonging an agony the real people in the North of Ireland had to endure for far too long.

Chapter Three

From 'Pieds Noirs' to Partners-in-Peace

Ruairí Ó Brádaigh paid a strange back compliment to the Reverend Ian Paisley in the late 1970s. The ex-IRA Chief of Staff is reported to have told a gathering of republicans that when their war was won and the Brits were gone the Provos would erect a statue of the Democratic Unionist leader right in the centre of Crossmaglen.

It seemed an odd promise to make; to commemorate Paisley in stone deep in the heart of Provo territory. After all, Paisley had long been a figure of fear and loathing in equal proportion within the Northern Catholic population, republican and non-republican alike. But Paisley's notoriety as the big bad Prod bogey-man was exactly Ó Brádaigh's point. The future founder of Republican Sinn Féin (which emerged in 1986 as a result of a split in Sinn Féin) pointed out to his audience that the Big Man was arguably the most effective recruitment sergeant for the Provisionals. Because every time it seemed he opened his mouth and bellowed out a chorus of anti-Irish/anti-Catholic vitriol, more ordinary nationalists would rush into the embrace of the republican movement. Paisley therefore embodied the Provos' conviction that unionism was un-reformable, reactionary, bigoted and intransigent.

What Ó Brádaigh could never have dreamt up, though, even in the wildest of his nightmares, was the sight that greeted the faithful readers of the republican newspaper *An Phoblacht/ Republican News* on 10 May 2007. Republicans (or, as Ó Brádaigh would now argue, 'ex-republicans') had finally elevated Paisley into their pantheon of honour.

The paper that once boasted the exploits of the Provisional IRA in its so-called 'War News' section published a full-page photograph of a smiling Ian Paisley alongside Martin McGuinness. The headline above spelt out in capitals an unmistakeable message: 'A GOOD DAY FOR IRELAND.' Paisley was suddenly transformed into one of the good guys.

The unlikely duo on the front of *An Phoblacht/Republican News* were standing in the Great Hall of Stormont two days earlier surveying the re-launch of a Northern Ireland Power-Sharing government headed up by the two forces that had wreaked so much division and, in the Provos' case, death and destruction across the North, for three decades.

Inside the paper, the ceremony to mark the elevation of Ian Paisley to First Minister and Martin McGuinness as his deputy was reported under the heading: 'Savouring a moment in history.' Written by *An Phoblacht/Republican News* correspondent Laura Friel, it was a sugary ahistorical and repetitive account of the incredible scenes unfolding at Stormont.

Friel felt that for those inside 'we were standing on the threshold of a new era'. She made back-references to the 'years of endeavour and sacrifice with the memories of those who could not stand beside us but whose contribution made the day possible'. Suddenly we were 'on the threshold [that word again] of a really big adventure, into a future full of the possibilities of human endeavour [repeated again]. And Stormont, that great edifice of the past, transformed.'

If some of 'those who could not stand beside us' had indeed been present as spectres at the feast or if they could contact the living through a medium and were able to speak, one wonders what they actually would have said. An entire generation had been raised through the Troubles to look upon not only Paisley but the entire Unionist political class as at best the dupes of British imperialism or at worst sectarian hate-mongers winding up the loyalist murder machines. Now these ghosts along with all the living were being told that these same Unionist leaders, many of whom had been in prime political positions since the Seventies, were equal partners in peace.

However, it wasn't just the Unionist political leadership that had been stereotyped for so long as a cabal of bowler-hat wearing, sweating and roaring sectarians. From the genesis of the Troubles in 1969 right up until arguably the 2006 St Andrews Agreement, the entire unionist population was portrayed as a mass of reaction, bad faith and false consciousness. Indeed the origins of the 1969 split in the republican movement that led to the Provisionals' formation are heavily coloured by Northern Catholic attitudes to the unionist community.

Those opposed to the leftward drift within the republican movement during the 1960s included men and some women living in Northern Ireland who had neither forgiven nor forgotten past unionist crimes visited upon nationalists, many of whom saw themselves trapped inside an illegal and hostile state. So when in 1969 the loyalist assault on Catholic homes along the 'borderlands' between the Falls and Shankill areas of Belfast erupted, these recalcitrant republicans were delivered a God-sent opportunity. All the fears and suspicions about unionism historically latent within the Northern Catholic community appeared to have been confirmed when Protestant mobs started burning homes in Bombay Street. The nascent Provisionals like IRA veteran Billy McKee or the Drumms played brilliantly on this psyche. Only the Provos could now prevent Catholics 'being murdered in our beds', the latter phrase a mantra oft repeated in the nationalist community in points of crisis in the Northern state.

At the beginning of the Troubles it was a tactic also employed in the Provos' power struggle with those they had broken away from, the Official IRA. Under the leadership of Cathal Goulding, the IRA pre-1969 had adopted a Marxist-Leninist strategy known as the 'Stages Theory'. Instead of headlong and ultimately disastrous armed conflict with the Northern Ireland state, the republican movement was urged to help reform it. By joining and becoming the vanguard of the Northern Ireland Civil Rights Movement, republicans could build bridges with progressive sections of the Protestant working class while working to undermine the Unionist political establishment and ultimately create a momentum towards Irish unity and even a Workers' Republic.

To the hard men from the mean streets of Belfast like Billy McKee and old comrades such as Gerry Adams Senior (the father of the future West Belfast MP), this line was dangerously flawed and entirely naive. For them the Protestants were privileged members of a 'labour aristocracy' who were supine servants of the British Crown. The 'Stages' strategy was the work of armchair theoreticians, they argued, unaware of the realities of Belfast and other parts of the North. The IRA's job first and foremost in the North of Ireland, the likes of McKee contended, was to protect the Catholic community. A much more negative analysis of this imperative was given as far back as the 1930s by former IRA man and founder of the leftist Republican Congress Peadar O'Donnell. He famously quipped that the IRA did not have a battalion of republicans in Belfast but rather a 'battalion of armed Catholics'.

What Peadar O'Donnell was heavily alluding to here was the 'Defenderist' tradition within Northern nationalism that stretched all the way back to the eighteenth century when the Catholic Defenders, a communal defence force against the rising Orange Order, allied with the utopian ideologues of the United Irishmen. While the United Irish movement talked about the 'unity of Catholic, Protestant and Dissenter', the Defenders had other, more visceral concerns — the defence of the besieged Catholic communities surrounded by a sea of Protestants and loyalists. Two centuries later it appeared nothing much had changed in the sectarian body politic of north-east Ireland.

The tension between the rhetoric of the United Irishmen and the reality of sectarian communal defence didn't just run through the increasingly divided republican movement. Emerging leaders of constitutional nationalism and eventual founders of the SDLP Paddy Devlin and Gerry Fitt even travelled to Dublin in the late summer of 1969 demanding the Irish government intervene militarily to protect Belfast's Catholics, or at least provide the beleaguered Catholic populace with the guns to defend themselves. (Fitt in the latter end of his life went to court to try to disprove the story and claimed he was defamed.)

The new 'defenders' of embattled Catholics got their chance for revenge for Bombay Street in the summer of 1970 in a battle that would supposedly wipe away the shame of the IRA appearing to be weapon-less and impotent in the face of loyalist mobs the previous year.

On 27 June 1970 a fierce gun battle broke out in the lower end of the Newtonards Road, one of the main thoroughfares through east Belfast. It occurred while thousands of Orangemen and their supporters were returning from a rally in central Belfast. The shooting, which lasted six hours, was concentrated around St Matthew's Chapel, the parish church of the Catholic enclave of Short Strand. It was the first sustained military action by Provisional IRA snipers and by the end of that day five Protestants and one Catholic had been shot dead. A further twenty-six people were wounded.

The origins of the clashes are still to this day a matter of bitter dispute. What matters more perhaps was the retrospective myth-making the Provos engaged in during its aftermath. Founding fathers of the PIRA such as Billy McKee were actively involved in the battle. They later portrayed their actions as a form of communal self-defence; they had prevented thousands of Protestants from swamping a small, vulnerable Catholic district. Finally it seemed Belfast's Catholics were no longer on their knees; they had arisen!

UVF veterans alongside Protestant residents of the lower

Newtonards Road area insist to this day that the first shots fired actually came from the republican side, i.e. towards the direction of the loyalist marchers. The loyalists claim that there was deliberate provocation, possibly even a conspiracy to foment a sectarian mini-crisis around the Catholic enclave, thus providing the Provisionals with a means to portray themselves as the defenders of a besieged nationalist people. Whatever the veracity of either theory, the myth of the Provos as the last resort halting total annihilation at the hands of bloodthirsty loyalist mobs became deeply embedded in the Belfast working-class Catholic psyche. And a myth it certainly was, given the huge level of casualties among the Catholic working class in the city from the time the Provos went on the offensive right up until the ceasefires of the 1990s.

Myth is the correct and apposite word to describe the legend that sprung up out of the blood-letting near the grounds of the Catholic church at the bottom of the Newtonards Road. In reality the PIRA was no more able to defend the Catholic population of the city than the pre-split IRA was back in the summer of 1969. In fact their actions prompted loyalist counter-violence all over Belfast. Twenty-four hours after the 'Battle of St Matthew's', around five hundred Catholic workers were expelled 'in revenge' from Harland and Wolff, the shipyard in sight of the Short Strand which had built the ill-fated *Titanic*.

Indeed within the enclave that was to become a major stronghold for the Provos, Catholics were still unsafe — even from the actions of republicans who were meant to defend them. Just under two years after the 'Battle of St Matthew's' eight people were killed when an IRA bomb exploded prematurely in Anderson Street in the Short Strand. Four of those who died were IRA members, the remaining four were civilians. In total around fifty houses were damaged in the massive explosion, which left a crater in the street and tossed at least one body 100 yards into the air. The bomb at Anderson Street remains the single biggest loss of life inflicted on the Short Strand community throughout the Troubles. Not even loyalist sectarian murder gangs, despite all their efforts through three decades, could match the carnage visited upon that small, tightly knit area in one single day. In a tragically ironic twist it turned out that one of the young IRA men to die in the blast had been involved in the St Matthews battle two years before. Seventeen-year-old Joseph Fitzsimmons was described in the republican publication *Belfast Graves* as an 'ammunition runner' for Billy McKee and his men during the shooting.

The Provisionals' clever and highly cynical exploitation of old Northern defenderist ideology was also in part about historic unfinished business. Not so much the unfinished business of 1916 and the 'betrayal' of partition five years later. Instead in its early years some of the movement's leading figures reached back far deeper into the past, right back to the sixteenth century.

One of the Belfast republicans who led the revolt against the Goulding-leadership and the IRA's new direction at the end of the 1960s was Liam Hanaway, a veteran activist from the Kashmir area off the Falls Road. Hanaway was part of what one RUC Special Branch officer later described as the 'network of families', many related through blood or marriage, that formed up the initial core of the Provisionals across Belfast, in particular the west of the city.

In late 1970/early 1971 two American journalists arrived in west Belfast to try and reach the new rebel army emerging in the city. The result of their stay was *Patriot Graves*, a photo-essay published by Follett Publishing House in Chicago.

The book captures the anarchy of the time — there are dramatic pictures of riots, IRA gun lectures in cramped terraced houses, armed Provos patrolling the streets. In all, the work is a piece of pro-IRA hagiography dressed up as objective photo-journalism and reportage. The dead give-away is in the dedication at the start — the book is in honour of Liam Hanaway.

It is supremely ironic too that the authors also quote in the book from Dominic Behan's 'The Patriot Game', his song penned after the disastrous border campaign of 1956–62. As the brother of the more famous playwright Brendan, Dominic insisted throughout the rest of his life that 'The Patriot Game' was a call to peace and not arms. The song, he would say to anyone prepared to listen to him, actually reflected on the futility of the violence rather than its supposed glory. Unsurprisingly Dominic Behan sided with the Officials in the split with the Provisionals at the advent of the Troubles.

Whilst it is coloured deeply green with pro-IRA propaganda, *Patriot Graves* none the less gives a very early and valuable insight into the way the sectarian divisions of the North influenced how the Provos saw their unionist neighbours. In an interview, some time in the spring of 1971, Liam Hanaway makes clear that the unionists are a foreign presence in their land.

'We had to contend with the Ulster Plantation that took place 400 years ago, which was mainly in the north-east. And many people have been instilled with the idea that we are descendants of the English, which we are not. But many still contend they are Britons, and wave a Union Jack. However, in spite of the propaganda down through the centuries, this country is slowly but surely moving towards a Republic.'

The authors follow Hanaway and others throughout 1971 and shortly after Internment they go back to the man they are clearly deeply impressed by. This second interview with Hanaway deals in large part with how republicans view how the unionists would react to a British withdrawal...and presumably an IRA victory.

'. . . Some people say that we will have a Unionist backlash. And it is possible that we would have the extreme political Unionists in opposition to the armed forces of the Republic. That's something which I wouldn't want. But let's face up to the fact that it's possible to see such a situation. But even so, I have no doubt that we would be able to control the situation in a very short time.'

His response was a common one heard from Provos when the subject of the loyalist reaction to withdrawal came up in conversation throughout the 1970s: that the Protestants might rebel but ultimately the forces of the Republic would quell any counter-revolution. There was no room back then in their calculations as to the true human cost of such a confrontation. Nor any comprehension as to how they could convince the unionists and loyalists to become 'true' Irishmen and women once their British masters had pulled down the last Union flag and got on the boat back to England. In a sense why would they have bothered to think through the consequences? After all, if the loyalists were the descendants of 'illegal occupiers' via the Plantation (in leftist radical chic terms, no different in fact from the Israeli settlers on the West Bank) then why worry about what the 'Prods' might think about a United Ireland or the new Republic?

For most volunteers at the time and certainly those who were confronted on the issue even among their cheerleaders in academia and media-land, the unionists were simply guilty of 'false consciousness'; if they didn't know what was good for them, then they could get out and go back to Scotland. Crude as this 'solution' to the Protestant Question seems now, one can recall hearing it proffered time and time again right up until the late 1980s, even from some of those who purported to be left wing.

None the less, for those still paying lip service to the central tenet of Wolfe Tone's philosophy ('the unity of Catholic, Protestant and Dissenter'), appeals to the politics of millennial revenge, to the imperative of reversing the Plantation two centuries before the United Irish movement emerged, seemed crudely sectarian; there had to be a more subtle approach therefore to the 'unionist problem'.

For the young men emerging into leadership positions in the late 1970s, many of them graduating from the 'University of Long Kesh', the language of chic anti-imperialism was deployed in their efforts to dismiss the unionists as a non-people.

At the end of that decade and up until the mid-1980s, *Magill* magazine became a critical organ through which the IRA amplified its message to wider Irish and international society. Sean O'Callaghan, one of the most important of the IRA 'pentiti', recalls that senior RUC Special Branch officers who spent hundreds upon hundreds of man hours debriefing him, regarded the annual Sinn Féin and IRA interviews in *Magill* as useful indicators of where the Provos were going next.

'One Branch man I knew used to wonder where in Belfast they could get *Magill*. He said there used to be a blind panic at RUC headquarters whenever the interviews came out to get their hands on them so that the force could analyse what the Provos were saying,' O'Callaghan remembers.

Even as late as the 1980s the Provos' attitude towards unionists was also linked to their struggles, intellectual and political, against their old rivals in the Officials, newly evolved fully by 1982 into The Workers Party. Thus while the Workers Party preached workers' unity and had already begun an outreach programme to Protestants in the North, Sinn Féin and the Provisionals needed to portray the unionist/loyalist community as irreformable reactionaries and the immovable allies of British imperialism.

Take the July 1983 *Magill* interview conducted by Michael Farrell with two representatives of the Provisional IRA leadership. In the same edition Farrell also interviewed Gerry Adams. There is a telling remark about the nature of the Protestants of north-east Ireland during a discussion between Farrell and the IRA over continued Provo attacks on indigenous members of the British Security Forces in Northern Ireland. One of the IRA spokesmen argues:

'Many loyalists have a supremacist mentality like the Afrikaaners in South Africa, the Pieds Noirs in Algeria or the Israelis. They have not the same privileges but the mentality is the same.'

This is Gael versus Planter dressed up in trendy garb for the twentieth century; the ancient struggles of Ireland's past glossed over with a red tint of Third World anti-imperialist rhetoric. It also sought to put the IRA on the same par as the Algerian NLF, the ANC and the PLO. Furthermore, the demonisation of the unionists as Ireland's equivalent to the Settler-Zealots on the West Bank or the descendants of the Boers in the Orange Free State served a useful purpose: it provided a moral basis, from a leftist viewpoint, for physical attacks on that community.

In the same interview, the IRA leaders issued this warning to those who might stand against the coming United Ireland: 'Anyone who opposes Irish self-determination with force will have to be met with force.'

The interview was conducted just weeks after Sinn Féin's key breakthrough in the British general election, the victory of Gerry Adams over Gerry Fitt in West Belfast.

Farrell complements his chat with the IRA with a parallel discussion with Adams. The Sinn Féin President also picks up the theme of the irreformable unionists: 'The unionist working class have no reason to move away from their present position.'

In a subliminal jibe at the Workers Party, Adams refers to sectarianism: 'The sectarian divisions are caused and maintained by the British. They [presumably the unionist workers] have marginal privileges and the unionist ruling class have significant privileges. You have to get rid of the prop which causes the sectarianism and in that new situation working class unity can be built.'

It is worth remembering that Adams at that time was unsuccessfully competing with the Workers Party for support in the working class redoubts of Greater Dublin. The *Magill* 1983 articles try to portray Adams and Sinn Féin in benign neo-left light. In his article Farrell concentrates on the new socialist and feminist agendas taking hold in the party. Some way round though still had to be found to get over the rather awkward fact that the party's military wing was engaged in killing Protestants North of the border, albeit in the main those who were members of the Royal Ulster Constabulary and the Ulster Defence Regiment. These policemen and soldiers had to be painted therefore as mere allies or at the very best dupes of British colonial rule. The struggle to force them into a United Ireland was thus not undemocratic after all given that a) they were shoring up an illegal state and b) they were the agents of the occupying power. The battle therefore was as legitimate as that of the FLN, ANC or PLO.

Adams closes his reference to the unionists with this imperative: 'We have to break the loyalist veto.' In other words the view accepted by every other political party in nationalist Ireland — that there could be no constitutional change without unionist consent — was a chimera. In the view of the IRA, unionist refusal to consent equalled an illegal veto on a supreme national right. It is important to remember this when observing Sinn Féin's evolution over the next few decades. Moreover, as opposed to the Workers Party, Labour in the North would, to borrow from that infamous of phrase of Eamon de Valera's, simply have to wait.

The Provisionals' project has often been described as the 'politics of illusion', but it was also, internally, the politics of self-delusion. Among the rank and file as well as the jail-educated leadership emerging in the North, there was a psychological need not to be branded in any way sectarian or have the 'struggle' perceived in that manner. One way of tarting up the violent campaign, which in real terms was wreaking social havoc and solidifying sectarian division, was to portray it as some kind of Latin American style struggle for liberation.

The Catholic hierarchy and the majority of its priests were throughout the Troubles resolutely opposed to the IRA's campaign of violence. Some senior clergymen did express sympathy on a human level for the plight of prisoners, most notably the late Cardinal Tomás Ó Fiaich, who compared the H-Blocks to the slums of Calcutta. (It is odd that Ó Fiaich was never upbraided resolutely enough for this comparison. The poor and destitute of Calcutta after all had no choice about being trapped in a life of grinding poverty and squalor; the Blanketmen chose to engage in dirty protests covering themselves and their cells in excrement in protest over the foolish policy of removing their political status.)

None the less even a strong nationalist with deep roots in republican South Armagh such as Tomás Ó Fiaich vigorously and consistently condemned the 'armed struggle' as both immoral and utterly counter-productive and divisive. After the Enniskillen massacre, for instance, the late Cardinal apologised on behalf of Ireland's four million Catholics to the Protestant people.

There was, however, a small band of priests who took a much more sympathetic view at least to the Provo analysis and their reasons for being at 'war'. Among them was the Fermanagh priest Fr Joe McVeigh, who penned a pamphlet in 1985 which attempted to graft South American Catholic Liberation Theology onto the Irish 'struggle'. In *British Occupation: The Role of the Church in Ireland*, Fr McVeigh writes:

> 'The Irish people's struggle for freedom from British military rule should be seen in the context of the struggles of many other oppressed people's seeking freedom from military rule and a say in their own affairs. It is another example of what Gustavo Gutierrez, a noted liberation theologist from Peru, refers to as the "eruption of the poor".'

Throughout the text there are other Latin American references, including the murdered Archbishop Romero of El Salvador. Even James Connolly, the Edinburgh-born Marxist and atheist, gets a theological make-over. Fr McVeigh quotes the historian and biographer James Beresford-Ellis, who described Connolly as 'one of the staunchest defenders of spiritual values in a world hell bent on materialism'. One wonders what a dialectical materialist like Connolly would have thought about being 'spiritualised' in this fashion, but what it does demonstrate is the way attempts were made through the Troubles to fuse Catholic-nationalism with radical Third World anti-imperialism.

The parallels drawn between the plight of the truly impoverished *campesinos* in Peru and Colombia with a working class in large part socially shored up by generous

British welfare payments are absurd. Leaving that aside, no matter how bad British state human rights violations were, especially in the early phase of the conflict, they do not begin to compare with the record of the us-backed military dictatorships that dominated South and Central America in the twentieth century. The Brits didn't round up political opponents in Windsor Park and execute them on the football field by the thousands as Pinochet's forces had done in Santiago. (It is worth adding too that when Britain went to war over the Falklands in 1982, republicans of all hues backed the Argentine Junta, a vile dictatorship that like all tyrannies invaded the islands as a populist distraction from its crimes and human rights abuses at home. The British defeat of that Junta precipitated its fall and ultimately the restoration of democracy!)

As for the 'eruption of the poor', while the foot soldiers of the 'armed struggle' in urban areas certainly emerged from ghettoes blighted by years of neglect and unionist discrimination, in rural communities many of the Provisionals' leading cadres came from relatively well-to-do farming backgrounds. Travelling through republican redoubts in parts of Tyrone and South Armagh, with their big houses, it was hard to equate all of this with Fr McVeigh's 'eruption of the poor'. These men, some of them living today in Southfork-style bungalows and mini-ranches along the Louth/Armagh border, were fired by something far less banal than poverty: they were fuelled instead by the politics of rural revenge (an uncauterised historic wound in the Ulster psyche) combined with an historic zeal to reclaim land that they believed was once theirs.

It wasn't just Adams though or indeed the man in the

balaclava who dismissed unionism as an equal partner in any solution to the Irish Question; the capacity of unionists to resist the rapid end of the Union and incorporation into an Irish Republic was treated with contempt by some of the Provos' British allies. In a 1984 edition of *Magill*, Adams's chief ally in the UK offered his very own 'Nescafé' instant solution to the conflict across the Irish Sea.

In an interview with Olivia O'Leary, Lord Mayor of London Ken Livingstone said he wanted disengagement done in less than a fortnight: 'I'd do it in ten days,' Livingstone boasted, 'rather than any gradual process of disengagement.'

Red Ken clearly had no fears that in that ten-day period the loyalists would be in any real trouble. In fact, he tells O'Leary he would be prepared to stay in west Belfast for the duration of the British pull-out.

'The Protestant terrorists wouldn't get involved in a civil war. They would know that the international forces would stop them. The very balance of terror between the two sides would stop such a war and the Irish could all get down to working out a constitution, a new deal, which Protestants would be quick to have a major say in.'

Note the key words here 'Protestant' and 'Irish' and the absence of another — unionist. The implication is that the Protestants are really Irishmen and women but don't really know it yet. In a sense this is no different than the attitude of the ultra-left towards the Israelis. During the 1970s, when the Palestinian kaffiyah became a must-have accessory in the wardrobe of every leftist from London to LA, the PLO promoted the idea of a Palestinian state where Jews, Muslims and Christians shared one identity. In it there was no room for any Israeli nation. The Jews, like everybody else from the Mediterranean to beyond the Jordan, were Palestinians — even if the Jews didn't know it yet either! This formula appealed to Western leftists everywhere because it got over the rather awkward question about what would happen to Israelis if the PLO and the Arab states ever won their war and marched finally into Tel Aviv victoriously, or in the case of the present Iranian President, left the coastal Israeli city in a smouldering, nuclear-polluted ruin. They could no longer afford in the propaganda war to talk about throwing the Jews into the sea, even if this was still what they promised to their own masses when their Western allies and apologists weren't looking and listening. Instead the vanquished Israelis would become good little Jewish citizens of a secular, maybe even socialist Arab state. The scales would fall from their eyes. They would finally realise they were Palestinians after all.

So it was with the unionists, the poor deluded Prods led astray by their cynical imperialist masters in London and the 'Big House' aristocrats and industrialists of Ireland's north-east corner. In the universe of Ken Livingstone, they too would surely come to their senses and understand where their true allegiances lay.

Olivia O'Leary, to her credit, was having none of this particular Livingstonian fantasy about acquiescent Prods wakening up suddenly and realising they were as Irish, after all, as Gerry Adams or Martin McGuinness. Wondering if she would stay with Livingstone in Andersonstown to enjoy these last ten days of British rule in Ireland, she replies acidly to Red Ken:

'Not on your life, I told him — not even for a free vegetarian dinner. I'd rather be in London on a subsidised bus where comment is free and diet is a political statement and peace is not maintained by a balance of terror.'

Whilst in Cage 11, Long Kesh, Gerry Adams emphasised to comrades how he was deeply influenced by one particular book: Michael Farrell's *The Orange State*. This work, alongside Franz Fanon's *Wretched of the Earth* and *The War of the Flea*, became a must-read publication for any republican revolutionary inside or outside the prison system, North and South. The basic premise of Farrell's book was that the Northern Ireland state was the bastard-child of an imperialist con trick, an illegitimate and, more importantly, irreformable entity with in-built sectarian bias against Catholics. Many of those who spent time with Adams during his incarceration recall that the future leader of the republican movement would implore them to read *The Orange State*.

Within the broad and often fractious republican family there was a deep-seated fear of loyalism and loyalists as well as dismissive contempt for them. In the mid-1970s, particularly after the Ulster Workers' Strike successfully brought down the first power-sharing executive, that communal anxiety was at its height. Even the Provisionals' leftist allies in People's Democracy constantly played up fears that a sectarian apocalypse was just around the corner. In the May 1975 edition of *Unfree Citizen*, for example, in an article mainly focusing on support for the British Troops Out movement, PD got very militant about the loyalists:

'The immediate threat facing the Catholic working class in the north is of a fascist take-over. The withdrawal of British troops could be only a prelude to that take-over unless that withdrawal is FORCED by the combined resistance of northern and southern workers against imperialism and loyalism . . .'

The same article then called for a blocking of military aid and trade to any new fledgling loyalist statelet. The organisation also called on all republican forces, including those that were killing one another in a series of feuds, to unite against the coming loyalist putsch.

'We call for co-operation between all the anti-imperialist military organisations, the PIRA and OIRA, the Revolutionary Citizens Army and the PLA and the various defence groups to mount united resistance to loyalist assaults.'

It ended with this prophetic warning, another classical Trotskyist end-of-days portent:

'The crisis in the North is nearing its climax.'

In the stormy atmosphere of mid-1970s Northern Ireland, such concerns were in large part perfectly understandable given the level of slaughter on the streets and the fact that the state seemed to lurch from crisis to crisis in just three years. Moreover, the loyalist paramilitary groups were inflicting almost daily acts of blatant sectarian butchery on vulnerable Catholics. Their so-called 'terrorise the terrorists' strategy was in reality the terrorisation of an entire community.

It was a commonly held view, not just one shared by the political actors and military activists, that the North was on the inevitable slide towards civil war. None the less it is clear that in the power struggles within their own community, first against the Officials and latterly and more crucially directed against the SDLP, the Provisionals both exploited and were aided by the ever looming threat of loyalist sectarian attack. This mirrored what was happening on the unionist side, especially among extreme elements such as Ian Paisley's DUP, which also exaggerated the threat of communal disaster and political sell-out for their own selfish party ends.

What has to be said, however, is that there also appeared to be important boundaries to all this manipulation, even in the darkest days of the Troubles. The capacity for Beirut-style mass atrocities, with hundreds of civilian deaths on a near daily basis, was clearly there all the time. None the less the Provisionals and their loyalist enemies by and large avoided the temptation to push Northern society over the abyss and plunge the state into a Lebanese-style outright civil war.

By the mid-1970s the Provisionals' mainly Dublin-based leadership had in fact been searching for ways to 'solve' the Protestant/unionist question beyond the 'boat people option' favoured by so many of their Northern grassroots activists and supporters. Dáithí Ó Conaill, one of the leaders of the rebellion against Cathal Goulding's new departure, was instrumental in drawing up the 'Éire Nua' document, a blueprint for a new Ireland based on de-centralising power to the island's four ancient provinces. In the Ireland of 'Éire Nua' there would be four regional parliaments, including one for a nine-county Ulster which Ó Conaill passionately believed would allay Protestant fears about being absorbed into a centralist, unified and Catholic-dominated state. 'Éire Nua' was federalist in nature and envisaged a near autarkic arcadia with heavy emphasis on indigenous Irish industries and the promotion of small farming — an economic formula which its critics labelled 'Gaelic Albania'. (The allusion to Albania might have been too kind; other cynics quipped that 'Éire Nua' meant 'Gaelic Cambodia-Year Zero'.)

The one aspect of 'Éire Nua' that did garner some

favourable coverage in the media and generated debate even within the fringes of unionism was its plans for devolving key powers to Ulster, albeit one now with a small in-built nationalist majority. While the architects of the policy like Ó Conaill and the then President of Sinn Féin Ruairí Ó Brádaigh were enthusiastic about its potential to woo unionists, 'Éire Nua' was deeply unpopular among those republicans who were on the front line — the Northern activists and members. In 1981 the new Northern cadre emerging into leadership positions — Gerry Adams, Martin McGuinness and Danny Morrison for instance — sought to overturn federalism. At the Ard Fheis that year Morrison denounced the policy as a 'sop to loyalism' and argued that 'you will have as much trouble getting the loyalists to accept a nine-county parliament as you will in getting them to accept a United Ireland, so why stop short?' The Northerners, who had cut their political teeth on the war-torn streets of Belfast and Derry, often facing not only the British army but also the armed loyalist groupings, believed they had a more realistic take on the true nature of unionists compared to the romantic Southern-based republicans. Indeed Morrison, who at that same conference uttered the notorious phrase 'a ballot paper in this hand and an Armalite in the other', in an interview with *Magill* three years later dismissed the unionist population as 'sectarian, almost racist'.

Adams and the Northern coup plotters saw federalism as the weak flank of the traditionalist Southern-based leadership. Although they failed on that occasion to gain a two-thirds majority needed to overturn the 'Éire Nua' policy, they didn't give up. A year later, buoyed by electoral successes in Northern Ireland, first during the hunger strike with the election of Bobby Sands and subsequently Owen Carron to Westminster, and then Sinn Féin securing seats in the 1982 Assembly elections, the Northerners tried again. Better organised than the previous year and with support from old IRA veterans like John Joe McGirl, Adams and his faction pushed through a motion that effectively killed off 'Éire Nua' as the republican movement's policy. Four years later Adams had ousted Ó Brádaigh as Sinn Féin President and the party agreed to drop its boycott of Dáil Éireann.

Paradoxically, the dropping of 'Éire Nua' (the 'sop to loyalism') was a key stepping stone on modern Sinn Féin's road towards constitutional politics. It certainly undermined Ó Brádaigh and those traditionalists who held that to recognise one parliament, that of the 'Free State', was the slippery slope towards compromise and the objective acceptance of partition. 'Éire Nua's' demise is also crucial in highlighting how far the present Sinn Féin and IRA leadership were prepared to go in manipulating sectarian passions forged in the Northern conflict. Fear and contempt for the loyalist population were used as a cover for what was essentially an internal political power struggle within republicanism. The irony must surely not be lost on the likes of Ó Brádaigh today when he watches Martin McGuinness traipse behind Ian Paisley at every function the First and Deputy First Minister have to attend at Stormont. Here is a man who was part of a cabal, undoubtedly a very representative one of the rank and file back in the early 1980s, that once excoriated the Southern traditionalists for seeking a federalist accommodation with unionists, now sitting down in the twenty-first century inside a still unionist majority parliament. McGuinness et al had charged that

Ó Brádaigh, Ó Conaill and their supporters were naive in the face of loyalism's true, sectarian nature. Just as the first wave of Provisionals in their struggles with the Officials weren't shy of exploiting Catholic fears of annihilation back in 1969/70, so the new Northern leaders whose careers developed on the back of the armed campaign appealed to deep-seated distrust of unionists and unionism to usurp the likes of Ó Brádaigh and Ó Conaill sixteen years later. Now at the end of a long, eventful and arguably unfulfilled life, Ó Brádaigh can at least reflect that his 'solution' — ditched so ruthlessly in 1982 — envisaging a nine-county as opposed to six-county parliament, is in many ways just like the one currently being operated by men like Martin McGuinness in Belfast. In fact 'Éire Nua' is even less of a 'sop to loyalism' than the present arrangement at Stormont.

Attitudes towards unionism within the Provos appeared therefore to harden considerably post 'Éire Nua' as the Northern leaders attempted to flex their muscles and act macho in the face of charges of sell-out from the republican die-hards who walked out of the 1986 Ard Fheis. In the aftermath of its abandonment of abstentionism four years later, the Provos offered its base instead the bloodthirsty prospect of an intensified 'war' largely thanks to the largesse of Libyan dictator Colonel Gaddafi and the tonnes of weapons and explosives his regime exported to Ireland.

Part of the Provos' 'big push' was to launch large scale attacks on British military installations in border regions. According to Sean O'Callaghan, one of the key IRA activists in the frontier zone who opted to stay with the new Adams' leadership, East Tyrone commander Jim Lynagh, was hell bent on establishing 'liberated zones' across the border areas.

Lynagh and his East Tyrone brigade launched a series of sorties on military bases and police stations right up until 1987 when the IRA suffered its greatest defeat at the hands of the British since the War of Independence — the death of eight IRA men, including Lynagh, at Loughgall.

Caught in the middle of the crossfire in this campaign and sometimes directly in the cross-hairs of IRA gun sights were the border Protestants. The majority of casualties in the counties of Fermanagh and Tyrone in particular were members of the locally recruited Ulster Defence Regiment and the RUC, both full and part-time. To the community from which these police officers and soldiers came from, this campaign was perceived as sectarian and aimed at driving an entire people out of areas where they had roots dating back several centuries. Regardless of how many times the Provisionals, their political spokespersons, their apologists on the ultra-left and their sneaking regarders in the media and academia protested that this was simply a war against occupying Crown forces, the community that actually bore the brunt of this brutal campaign saw it in rather more pure black and white terms. In their analysis, it was designed to push them off the land and pen them further back away from the frontier into an ever-decreasing north-east pocket beyond the River Bann. This was a new land war fought with Kalashnikovs rather than pikes and swords.

In the 1980s the Provos and their spokesmen invented a chilling phrase to cover a wide range of victims, starting from British troops down to local businessmen supplying army bases, from serving police officers to workers repairing damaged security installations. 'Legitimate targets' became an elastic catch-all concept that acted as political camouflage for the Provisionals and a leadership anxious to avoid accusations that their campaign was nothing other than sectarian. And even if we were to accept the Provos' intent regarding the unionist population — that they never sought to deliberately target Protestants in the conflict — the net results of that campaign told a different story.

Even the targeting of members of the controversial locally recruited Ulster Defence Regiment was coloured by sectarian motivations. More than two hundred members of the UDR and later the Royal Irish Regiment combined were shot dead during the Troubles, the majority of them by the IRA. The overwhelming majority of them too were off duty at the time of their murders, i.e. 162 out of 204 killed. A fifth of them had already left the UDR when they were targeted. Most were not heavily armed or on patrol or inside fortified military installations when they died. They were in fact living in their communities, often at home, on their farms, driving school buses or delivering post. That also made them relatively soft targets.

They were gunned down in front of their wives, their children, their relatives, even their pupils and the school children they were driving to school. Moreover, those who shot them or placed bombs under their cars were in many cases able to move with ease to and fro across the border, relatively unimpeded by the security forces south of the frontier. In the minds of border Protestants in particular, these attacks were as sectarian and cynical, aimed at driving them off the land, as those the loyalist paramilitaries were directing against vulnerable Catholics in north Belfast.

Was it simply a coincidence that the massacre of eleven Protestants in a bomb attack on a Poppy Day commemoration

An IRA volunteer. (*Pacemaker Press International*)

Provisional IRA members on the Falls Road during the Sinn Féin march to Casement Park in 1979. (*Pacemaker Press International*)

An IRA mural in Coalisland, 1988. (*Pacemaker Press International*)

Tom Hartley, Ken Livingstone (then a Labour MP and later Mayor of London) and Gerry Adams on the Falls Road, 1983. (*Pacemaker Press International*)

The funerals of the Gibraltar three, Mairéad Farrell, Seán Savage and Danny McCann, 1988. (*Pacemaker Press International*)

Bobby Sands (*right*). (*Pacemaker Press International*)

A stark message in Andersonstown. (*Pacemaker Press International*)

Martin McGuinness, 1980. (*Pacemaker Press International*)

An early Sinn Féin election poster. (*Linen Hall Library*)

Martin McGuinness, Gerry Adams and Danny Morrison at the Bobby Sands commemoration march on the Falls Road, 1983. (*Pacemaker Press International*)

Gerry Adams and Brendan Hughes in Long Kesh in the 1970s. (*Press Eye*)

Gerry Adams with President Bill Clinton in the White House, St Patrick's Day, 2000. (*Getty Images*)

Veteran Republican Brian Keenan at the national Loughgall commemoration march in 2007. (*Press Eye*)

A mural on the Falls Road, Belfast, 2000. (*Pacemaker Press International*)

Bertie Ahern with USA Special Envoy, Mitchell Reiss, September 2005. (*PA Photos*)

Mary Lou McDonald in election mode. (*PA Photos*)

Gerry Adams and Donegal candidate Pearse Doherty, outside the GPO in
O'Connell Street, Dublin, launching the party's health manifesto for the 2007
general election. In what was a disappointing campaign for the party, Doherty
failed to win a seat in Donegal. (*PA Photos*)

Brendan Hughes in Belfast shortly before his death. (*Press Eye*)

The Northern Ireland Executive formed following the Belfast Agreement of 1988, with David Trimble as First Minister and Seamus Mallon as Deputy First Minister. (*Reuters*)

The funeral of Brendan Hughes, Belfast, February 2008. (*Pacemaker Press International*)

Tom Hartley, Sinn Féin Lord Mayor of Belfast, about to lay a wreath at the Belfast City Hall to commemorate Irish soldiers who died at the Battle of the Somme. (*Pacemaker Press International*)

The negotiations at St Andrew's in Scotland that produced the agreement that broke the long deadlock. (*PA Photos*)

The improbable ending: Ian Paisley and Martin McGuinness as First Minister and Deputy First Minister. (*Pacemaker Press International*)

in Enniskillen occurred in the same year as the IRA's border offensive was halted at Loughgall? While the slaughter in the heart of Fermanagh's capital on 8 November 1987 tore away the mask of so-called 'anti-imperialist' respectability from the face of the Provisional movement throughout the world, within this particular closed, besieged citadel of the unionist community it merely bolstered a widespread belief that the 'armed struggle' was directed at erasing them and their tradition entirely from the island of Ireland.

In many ways 1987 can be seen as the year of the beginning of the end for the armed campaign. The physical elimination of one of the IRA's most active units, combined with the international opprobrium its political wing had to endure after the Poppy Day massacre, were key signposts on the road to the ceasefire. Nor is it coincidental that in this same year Gerry Adams made his first overtures to Charles J. Haughey via the Clonard priests to help him chart a new, wholly political strategy. In the meantime the Provisionals continued prosecuting a campaign that the majority of Protestants in the frontier zone regarded as entirely sectarian.

Back in Belfast the new post 'Éire Nua' leadership were not shy either in cynically harnessing legitimate Catholic grievances to justify their own squalid campaign of sabotage and assassination. Even allegations of ongoing systematic and structured anti-Catholic discrimination were harnessed to legitimise crimes up to and including murder even when they occurred in havens of relative peace and neutrality.

On 7 December 1983 the IRA murdered one of the rising stars of the Ulster Unionist Party outside the library at Queen's University Belfast, where he worked as a law lecturer. Edgar Graham's cold-blooded murder right in front of the eyes of students was organised by an IRA intelligence officer who was himself a student at the very same university. What we now know about the killing thanks to the likes of Sean O'Callaghan was that the IRA in Belfast received external advice from academia suggesting Graham had the potential to become a formidable political foe. O'Callaghan, who as IRA Southern Commander had exclusive insight into the Provo leadership's thinking at the time, believes the organisation's high command decided that they couldn't allow for the emergence of an articulate, educated unionist leader in the making. One of the supreme ironies of the murder was that Edgar Graham's closest colleague on the campus was another law lecturer called David Trimble, a fellow UUP member and future leader of unionism who would have to sit down in government one day with the men that sanctioned the killing of his friend.

Almost exactly a year later Sinn Féin openly gloated over the Graham killing in *Iris* magazine, by the standards of the time a slickly produced glossy publication aimed mainly at selling the Provo line on Ireland to an international audience. In its December 1984 edition *Iris* ran a five-page feature focusing on allegations of anti-Catholic bias at Queen's University. Its author, one Peadar O'Torban, noted that although the university student population was now almost 50 per cent Catholic, the composition of the teaching staff was still overwhelmingly Protestant. O'Torban quoted statistics for the medical faculty that showed that not a single 'Irish Catholic' was head of any department. Overall, the *Iris* investigation found that of the ninety-four chairs on the campus only eight were held by 'Irish Catholics'.

The tone and character of the article is encapsulated in the

headline: 'Queen's University — Unionism's academic front.'
Beneath the banner headline there is barely concealed glee
that the Provos a year earlier had punctured the neutral space
of the university.

'A heightened sense of moral outrage is reserved for those
occasions when an IRA attack in the environs of Queen's
brings home a harsher perspective. Then, the IRA is accused
of "violating" an "academic haven" as though the university
exists totally divorced from the conflict.'

In other words Queen's and presumably Edgar Graham
had it coming to them, according to the twisted moral
universe of *Iris* and its writers.

On the penultimate page of the feature, where O'Torban
fumes and rages about the lack of Catholic lecturers, there is
an inset photograph (one assumes from either Queen's
University or the Ulster Unionists) of a youthful-looking
Edgar Graham superimposed above a much larger one of the
slain lecturer, a sheet covering his body, his briefcase still on
the ground where he died on that cold December morning.
The photo-caption beneath refers to the 'IRA's execution' of
the 29-year-old academic and it points out that Graham was
'the UUP's "law and order" spokesman, a leading advocate of
hired perjurers . . .'

Edgar Graham had to die therefore because a) he
supported the Supergrass system and b) he belonged to the
alleged academic wing of the so-called Orange State.

Beyond one's obvious moral outrage at such a revolting
apologia for murder, the article is nevertheless revealing in
what it says about the Provos' past exploitation of
sectarianism. It is no accident that the Graham murder is
dropped into a feature touching on long-standing, often

completely justified Catholic grievances about unfair employment practices and structural discrimination at work.

This is barely even innuendo. The heavy hint here is that terrorist acts, like the one that took Edgar Graham's life, were somehow inevitable simply because Catholics suffered discrimination. On reading this kind of specious logic one recalls again the words of the great nineteenth-century Land League leader Michael Davitt in his denunciation of agrarian violence as a response to the Great Famine:

'The people of Munster are starving. Will murder feed them?'

Throughout the Troubles and beyond to the final ceasefires, the Provisionals have howled to the heavens in protest every time they are faced with charges of sectarianism. Republicanism, as Danny Morrison once told the Unionist lawyer and former MP Robert McCartney in a televised debate between the two men in the early 1980s, is entirely secular. Morrison and others like him have constantly referred back to Wolfe Tone and the United Irishmen and the unity of Catholic, Protestant and Dissenter. Faced with the realities of Northern Ireland, however, such protests of filial love for their Protestant brothers and sisters were mere lip service to Tone and his late eighteenth-century band of Enlightenment Utopians. As the *Iris* article on Queen's demonstrates, when the Provos needed to appeal to the basest fears and (very often understandable) resentments of the Northern Catholic population they did so, in this case to contextualise this murder.

It is worth remembering finally when recalling the sordid nature of Edgar Graham's murder, and the need for the Provisionals to justify it twelve months later to a wider global audience, that there were others campaigning at Queen's to create a level playing field for Catholic students and academics, others who didn't resort to violence or provide succour or excuses for murder on campus or indeed anywhere else in their society. It is they who deserve the credit for battling against discrimination and fighting for equality rather than the murder gang or, worse still, those that played the whispering games that brought about death and further division to a university campus.

By the end of the 1980s it was clear to the republican strategists now firmly in control of the post Ó Brádaigh movement that they were trapped in a cul de sac; they had suffered electoral setbacks in the North and their strategy to extend political influence in the Republic was failing miserably. Even in that critical year of 1987 Adams had been in secret contact with Charles J. Haughey via the Redemptorist priests at Clonard Monastery with a view, unknown to the overwhelming majority of the 'volunteers', to find a way for republicans to reverse out of the dead end the armed campaign had driven them into. Although the contacts with Haughey produced little, the Clonard priests continued to pursue other channels for Adams, most importantly with the SDLP leader John Hume. Within the space of five years those contacts had led to the Hume-Adams talks, or as republicans like to put it, in order to emphasise who was really in charge, the Adams-Hume talks.

The Adams leadership talked up the prospect of constructing a 'pan-nationalist front' out of the dialogue with Hume. In the early 1990s such an alliance fuelled unionist fears further and poisoned an already toxic atmosphere during which the loyalist paramilitary forces also enjoyed a murderous revival. Throughout the period building up to the 1994 ceasefires the mantra the Provisionals deployed regularly in relation to unionists was the need for the British government to become 'persuaders'. That is, persuaders as to the inevitability of a United Ireland. Even at this late stage in the IRA's campaign, the Provisionals were still delivering the message to the wrong address. They were talking to the British establishment rather than the people on their doorstep. In the early Nineties the republican argument went that it was up to Britain to convince unionists that their future lay in a United Ireland rather than with the UK. All the while the IRA continued to devastate mainly Protestant towns with huge bombs and target Protestants serving or having even the most tenuous connections to the security forces. This was still the politics of fantasy land even if there was a dawning realisation from the leadership downwards that the IRA's 'armed struggle' had run its course.

During the build-up to the first IRA ceasefire on 31 August 1994, for instance, IRA fugitive and Sinn Féin spokeswoman Rita O'Hare briefed at least one UK correspondent on the republican movement's strategy post-cessation towards the unionist community. According to one correspondent who relayed the story to me later, the still-on-the-run, flame-haired IRA veteran informed him that the Provos intended to sow confusion and division within the ranks of unionism. The ceasefire, O'Hare asserted, would result in loyalism collapsing 'under the weight of its own contradictions'. This appeared to be the strategy when dealing with unionists up to and even beyond the signing of the Good Friday Agreement in Easter Week 1998. Gerry Adams seemed to give the game away too when at an internal party conference in

County Meath he reminded delegates about the efficacy of republican-led community protests against controversial Orange Order and Apprentice Boys' parades.

The loyal marching institutions fell for every single trap the republican movement laid down for them. The Orange Order and Apprentice Boys refused to talk to nationalist residents' groups in areas of contentious loyalist marches because the majority of them were headed up by former IRA prisoners with terrorist form. The loyal orders conveniently forgot the disproportionately high number of their members, especially in Greater Belfast, with links to loyalist paramilitary groups. Sinn Féin inspired community protest organisations easily won each individual propaganda battle, portraying the loyal orders as nothing more than downright hypocrites. It was a strategy hardly aimed at building confidence between the no-longer-at-war republican movement and the 'Prods'. Nevertheless in terms of whipping up sectarian passions and harvesting the votes of nationalists quite justifiably outraged over Orange hypocrisy and its crass sectarianism, it was an entirely effective strategy.

In the pre and early post ceasefire period the IRA also misread the intentions of the loyalist paramilitary forces. Back in 1991, during the failed Brooke Talks, the umbrella group representing the UVF and UDA, the Combined Loyalist Military Command, had called a temporary ceasefire. This, the CLM said, was to enable the talks to take place in an atmosphere of relative peace and in addition demonstrate that the loyalists were serious about supporting a settlement that would accommodate both unionists and nationalists. The mainstream republican leadership, already hostile to any deal that Sinn Féin was not central to, rejected overtures amplified across the media from the loyalists for the IRA to follow suit. Instead the Provisionals escalated their violence in early summer 1991 with a series of large scale bombing attacks on mainly Protestant towns across Northern Ireland. Violence would be applied as the Provos' very own 'veto' on political progress, and it appeared to work as the negotiations broke down amid recriminations and a resumption in loyalist terrorism as well.

From the referendum in May 1998 that ratified the Good Friday Agreement North and South of the border until David Trimble's final demise in the 2006 Westminster General Election, devolved government suffered a series of stop/go crises. At the centre of the instability was Trimble, the first unionist leader ever prepared to sign a deal that included the republican movement. And the main cause of that turbulence was the issue of IRA decommissioning. It would take seven years for the Provisonals to finally do what the then largest unionist party in that community asked them to deliver — putting the IRA's huge arsenal of weapons and explosives beyond use. The Provisionals used the prospect of decommissioning to extract as many concessions as they could gain out of the Blair administration. They even struck up a close rapport with Blair's Downing Street Chief of Staff, Jonathan Powell, who carried out a secret version of Kissingeresque shuttle diplomacy with the Provos, holding meetings with senior IRA commanders in backstreet houses in west Belfast.

A parallel strategy of de-stabilising and dividing loyalism was put into place. Indeed in the three years after the temporary 1991 cessation the loyalists, most notably the UVF leadership guided by the late David Ervine, transmitted messages across the front-line to their republican foes, even at times when loyalists were intensifying their assault on the entire nationalist community. The mantra that Ervine et al attempted to relay to republicanism was brutally simple: 'You stop, we stop.'

In the weeks leading to the Provisionals' ceasefire on 31 August 1994, the IRA intensified its attacks on loyalists, some of which were a case of score-settling, as in the assassination of UDA killers Joe Bratty and Raymond Elder in south Belfast, or, in the case of Ray Smallwoods, the removal of one of loyalism's few political strategists. Yet despite the onslaught, which also included bomb attacks on pubs frequented by UDA members in Belfast, loyalism's politico-military leadership moved towards their own ceasefire two months after the IRA's. Indeed, as the late David Ervine remarked shortly after the UVF and UDA cessation on 13 October 1994: 'The Provos wanted to strut the world stage as peacemakers while we, the bloodthirsty loyalists, were still killing people.'

The evolution of the Provisionals' attitude towards unionists and unionism (from hated Planter-usurpers, to false-conscious suffering Pieds Noirs, to the need-to-be-Persuaded and so on) is central in understanding why their overall political project has failed. Their split with the Officials at the start of the Troubles was in part a response to what was happening on the streets but also, quite critically, an ideological difference over how to approach the north-east Protestant population. The events of the summer of 1969 and subsequent loyalist assaults on the Catholic community appeared initially at least to confirm the Provisionals' analysis that not only was the state of Northern Ireland beyond reform but those that remained loyal to it were also beyond redemption, at least while they remained locked in their so-called 'imperialist mindset'. And yet after three decades of fighting to destroy the state and the union that these 'settlers' still loyally clung onto, the Provisionals acknowledged finally that these same people had to be listened to . . . even long before the British packed up and left for good.

Even before devolution was restored and the once unthinkable deal between the DUP and Sinn Féin became a reality, the Provisionals had embarked on an outreach programme to Protestants and unionists. The roots of it lay in small step initiatives involving the likes of Tom Hartley, a close friend of Adams in west Belfast, and Alex Maskey, the first nationalist Lord Mayor of Belfast, who was elected to the post in 2003. Indeed Hartley became so much a near permanent fixture at conferences organised at venues such as the liberal Presbyterian church at Fitzroy, south Belfast, that he gained the nickname 'The Provos' Special Ambassador to the Prods'. While the audience attending that church were arguably unrepresentative liberals compared to the wider Protestant community, Hartley and later Maskey would become central players in even more important initiatives aimed at building trust across traditional divides. Hartley became the first Sinn Féin representative to attend a ground-breaking Poppy Day commemoration at the British Legion memorial in Goldenbridge in Dublin. It was ground-breaking not only because of the presence of an Irish President, Mary McAleese, but also because of the fact that the Provisionals were finally acknowledging that the Irish war dead who fought and died for Britain in the two great conflicts of the twentieth century deserved, finally, to be remembered.

During his term of office Alex Maskey also laid a wreath at the cenotaph in Belfast City Hall on Remembrance Day — an act that would have been absolutely taboo just a few years earlier.

The irony of all this was surely not lost on Hartley and Maskey's old rivals in the Officials. They, along with then *Irish Times* columnist Kevin Myers, were among the first in the Republic to seek to highlight how important the legacy of the World Wars, especially the first Great War, was in the Ulster Protestant psyche. In the Workers Party theoretical journal *Workers Life*, Workers Party-aligned writers wrote about 'Ulster's 1916' and how the slaughter at the Somme had been burned into the north-east Protestant collective consciousness. These pioneering explorations of unionist history and culture took place in the 1980s when the Provisionals and their allies chose to dismiss the sacrifice at the Somme simply as a grand old imperialist con-trick or, as one ultra-leftist supporter of the 'armed struggle' termed it back then: 'Donkeys led by donkeys.' But what were once 'sticky heresies' during the Eighties would of course eventually become a 'genuine desire to outreach to the unionist community'.

Republican attempts to open dialogue and build bridges with the unionist community took on a more structured form as it became clearer, after the Northern Bank robbery and the murder of Robert McCartney, that Sinn Féin had nowhere to go except into the embrace of Ian Paisley's DUP. They even enlisted former IRA bomber and prisoner Martina Anderson to head up the Provos' new 'Love bomb the Prods' campaign. To date, however, no unionist with any credible support within that community, nor any liberal Presbyterian minister or academic, has been won over to the cause. And even if the Provos do succeed in securing a segment of Protestants to their belated United Ireland-by consent, it still illuminates how far they have departed from their philosophical roots. Paradoxically Sinn Féin cannot realise its goal of unity by 2016 (the 100th anniversary of the Easter Rising) or even further into the future without securing a considerable tranche of new Protestant votes in any future border poll. The 'Pied Noirs' of Ireland, their children and grandchildren now hold the key to reunification, as they have probably always done. On the unionist/Protestant question we are back then where Goulding et al started in the 1960s, in a twenty-first century version of the 'Stages Theory'. To argue otherwise is to dispute fundamental political realities.

Sinn Féin's latter day outreach programmes to the Protestant community (albeit conducted in a very patronising and paternalistic tone); the belated recognition of the tradition of 'Ulster's 1916' and how important it remains to unionists; and, most crucially of all, Sinn Féin's willingness to enter a power-sharing arrangement in a parliament still under the final sovereign control of the UK, mark a cataclysmic ideological reverse for Provisionalism. The events of the last decade and in particular the last two years in Northern Ireland confirm that ideological defeat. The Provisionals have reached the point of John Hume and the SDLP's 'Agreed Ireland'. The 'British Presence' is no longer regarded primarily as soldiers from Liverpool, Glasgow or London patrolling Irish streets who are commanded by political mandarins with plummy accents and public school educations. The 'British Presence' is now accepted (reluctantly and always in the face of protest) to mean (at least for mainstream republicans) those on the island of Ireland that still see themselves as British.

From Planters to Pied Noirs to Partners-in-Peace: it has been a long, serpentine, very often fascinating and in all probability inexorable path from the politics of no compromise towards the politics of power-sharing, but it is one nevertheless strewn with much blood and bitter, arguably lasting communal division.

Just under a month after those incredible scenes at Stormont on 8 May 2007 when devolution was restored, the Irish cricket team came calling to Parliament Buildings. Fresh from their success at the Cricket World Cup in the West Indies, the side were honoured for their endeavours — particularly that famous, unexpected victory against Pakistan — with an audience with the First and Deputy First Ministers. Martin McGuinness pointed out to the media gathered around them that many republicans he knew had always been cricket fans, albeit secret ones given the sport's long association with all things English. To mark the occasion McGuinness and Paisley were given a cricket bat each, both signed by the entire Irish squad. The images the next day were both jarring and bitterly ironic. A smiling Ian Paisley holding up a wooden bat: the last time he had done so in a public place was back in 1985 when he brought in a sledgehammer to a press conference at DUP headquarters and vowed to 'Smash Sinn Féin'. We will never know for sure if Deputy First Minister McGuinness ever wielded a piece of finely honed wood to transmit any hard-line political message. What we do know is that the movement he led for so long wasn't shy in using wooden batons and sticks in its campaign to keep 'anti-social elements' brutally in line within their own community.

More telling perhaps than the smiles and grins of two

men with wooden bats in their hands was Martin McGuinness's comments about the secret society of republican cricket lovers. Maybe the former IRA Chief of Staff turned Deputy First Minister was alluding to a fellow member of the Provisional Army Council and his one-time comments on the connection between cricket and imperialism.

Brian Keenan*, the dedicated Marxist-Leninist and admirer, ally and friend of Arab dictatorships who masterminded the Provos' bombing campaign in Britain, once issued this warning to a fellow inmate, the informer Sean O'Callaghan, about Perfidious Albion.

'Don't trust the English, they invented cricket,' Keenan is reputed to have told O'Callaghan while the two were incarcerated at Her Majesty's Pleasure. The incongruous sight of one of Keenan's 'two fine fucking Catholic boys' (as he once described Adams and McGuinness) with the cricket bat at Stormont surely underlined that old, gnarled revolutionary's worst fears, that the British were indeed very good at playing and indeed winning a long game. The 'English', as Keenan called them, had pushed the Provisionals into a position where they had accepted the principle of consent. In doing so they had lost the Long Game.

*Brian Keenan passed away after a long battle with cancer in early summer 2008.

Chapter Four
The Laughter of Our Children

All politicians love children, but in the totalitarian mindset the very young are not merely cute campaign backdrops at election time; rather they are weapons in the universal struggle both to control the past and in turn to shape the future.

Eastern European dissidents who lived under late communism best recognised and understood the rationale behind this political form of paedophilia, this abuse of the innocent to create a new 'Republic of Forgetting'.

Milan Kundera in his 1982 masterpiece novel *The Book of Laughter and Forgetting* identified this particular form of mass manipulation in the way the post-Prague Spring leadership under Gustav Husak used children.

There is a memorable passage towards the latter end of the book when Kundera describes a scene from Prague in the mid-1970s. It concerns Husak (Czechoslovakia's very own 'President of Forgetting') becoming an honorary young communist pioneer, an award bestowed on him by the children of the nation. "'Children, you are the future," Husak cries out from the platform. "Children, never look back.'"

In Kundera's view the regime re-imposed by Soviet tanks in 1968 wanted to erase the entire memory of a country, to wipe the slate clean after the Prague Spring and to use children as the means to rub out all traces of that recent uncomfortable past. They had no alternative. Husak and his comrades simply couldn't afford to let their people look back.

'. . . what he [Husak] meant was that we must never allow the future to collapse under the burden of memory,' Kundera noted. 'Children, after all, have no past whatsoever. That alone accounts for the mystery of charmed innocence in their smiles.'

Hitler once boasted to the remnants of the opposition in the Reichstag that the Nazi party no longer cared about them. Once in power, the Führer warned them, they would seize and mould their children, even the children of their bitterest opponents. Stalin too loved to be seen receiving bouquets of flowers and endless applause from little boys and girls for the benefits of the comrades and the cameras.

But it isn't just totalitarian regimes and dictatorships that endlessly use the very young in their propaganda and organised lies. Non-state political organisations that are run on similar lines of iron discipline, democratic centralism or quasi-military rule also tend to enlist children in their ideological battles . . . or, in the Provisionals' case, as cushions to soften the impact of numerous ideological somersaults.

In the current battle for Irish history, our very own mini 'President of Forgetting', Gerry Adams, and his loyal lieutenants have deployed the child as a weapon in their latest struggle to re-write the truth about the last four decades.

Hence in recent times the use and over-use of a phrase allegedly coined by Bobby Sands in the H-Blocks: 'Let our revenge be the laughter of our children.'

On the surface, this nine-word phrase appears to be as sentimental, twee and vacuous as a Hallmark greeting card message. Yet it carries out two important functions in post-ceasefire Ireland. Firstly, it is a tug at the heartstrings, an appeal to the ethereal and all that is good, i.e. children. The words try to capture or perhaps re-capture a time of innocence when children laughed and nightingales sang. It also throws a soft focus glow over the past gone by. Secondly, it is so intangible and airy that it creates a fog to cover a major political shift. Where once the volunteers fought, and sometimes died, for such concrete goals as a United Ireland or a 32-County Democratic Socialist Republic, now all the sacrifices and slaughter will be worth it in the end when we all return to the garden of our childhood, or alternatively to pastures new where kids can skip through Arcadian fields and laugh to their hearts' content.

In 2006 'the laughter of our children' echoed all over nationalist Ireland as Sinn Féin leaders tried to exploit the 25th anniversary of the 1981 hunger strike. It was a time not just for a nostalgic look back on that febrile, gloomy period in Northern Ireland's history. The ten men who died in the H-blocks were to be resurrected and, like the laughing children, become props in Sinn Féin's new project to achieve power in both states of Ireland.

Not everyone whose children actually died on the death fast twenty-five years earlier were happy with the way their sons were being transformed into moving backdrops behind Sinn Féin's seemingly unstoppable electoral bandwagon.

For a start, three out of the ten hunger strikers were not actually members of the IRA. They were in fact activists with the Irish National Liberation Army, an ultra-left break-away organisation from the Official IRA. The INLA trio were Patsy O'Hara and his fellow Derryman Michael Devine, alongside Kevin Lynch from Dungiven. O'Hara's and Devine's relatives were deeply opposed to the use of their loved ones in Sinn Féin's organised commemorations on the 25th anniversary. O'Hara's mother, Peggy, a devout Catholic, was and still is furious at the way her Marxist revolutionary son has somehow been adopted (more accurately hijacked) as a Sinn Féin icon.

Peggy O'Hara's front living room at her house in a pristine middle-class cul de sac on Derry's West Bank is a temple of contradictions. On some of the walls and tables are Catholic religious icons including the Sacred Heart of Jesus and his mother the Virgin Mary. On others there are portraits of her son, the bearded Italianate INLA bomb-maker who built the device that killed Margaret Thatcher's close friend, the Tory MP Aiery Neave in the Palace of Westminster in 1979. Alongside Patsy O'Hara's picture are images long connected to the INLA with its red stars, hammers and sickles, and clenched fists holding up Kalashnikovs — all in defiant revolutionary poses.

The octogenarian grandmother with the dyed black beehive hairstyle was and is an unlikely firebrand revolutionary. Yet during the 2007 Assembly election campaign she was fiercely adamant that her son's image should never be included in Sinn Féin literature, electoral or historical.

'My Patsy didn't die so that they [Sinn Féin] can walk into Stormont. He died for the republic. I hate it when I see

Patsy's face being used by them like that. I am certain that Patsy would have been opposed to any return to that place.'

This then was what motivated the mother of the INLA hunger striker to stand twelve months later against Sinn Féin in the elections to the Northern Ireland Assembly that led eventually to power-sharing being restored.

The exploitation of the hunger strike, the images surrounding the death fast as part of Sinn Féin's corporate image, also plunged mainstream republicans and their supporters into new depths of retail kitsch. In the United States, Noraid, the Provisionals' North American fund-raising arm, decided to commemorate the ten men who died on hunger strike with a plate. A New Jersey branch of Noraid charged 25 dollars plus seven dollars shipping for plates that displayed the pictures of all ten hunger strikers.

Peggy O'Hara's other son Tony had spent time in jail with Bobby Sands in 1978. When he saw the plate on the worldwide web complete with an image of his younger brother he was horrified.

'It was tacky in the extreme. But in a way I was not surprised because in America they will sell anything no matter how tacky to make money. The images of Patsy and other INLA men were hijacked a long time ago by the republican movement. What was unacceptable was that a group like Noraid, which has many right wing supporters in America, never liked the INLA because they were republican socialists. Yet they were using our Patsy and the other boys to sell this product.'

Tony O'Hara, who was released from the Maze shortly after the death of Mickey Devine, the last INLA prisoner on the fast and final hunger striker to die, recalled that both families had boycotted the Sinn Féin organised commemoration in Derry that year.

> 'They ignored the INLA prisoners' contribution to the H-Block struggle and refused to allow the commemoration to be a broad based committee.
>
> The republican movement's supporters in America at the time of the hunger strike, it's worth remembering, blocked fund-raising for the INLA prisoners. One Noraid supporter even tore up a cheque he had written to IRSP representative Sean Flynn when he said he supported black civil rights in America.
>
> Nor later was any money forthcoming from Irish-America to raise funds for a memorial to Patsy and Mickey in Derry City Cemetery and yet now Noraid is using the boys' image to sell a plate.'

Michael Devine's son, Michael Junior, was equally scathing about the way his father's death had been hitched to a new political bandwagon. 'My dad was a socialist republican who would have been opposed to the Stormont sell out and the type of conservative Americans supporting Sinn Féin.'

Richard O'Rawe, the IRA's press officer inside the Maze during the 1981 hunger strike, described the commemorative plate as 'totally inappropriate'. O'Rawe said: 'You eat food off a plate and yet they have brought out a plate to commemorate the men who died refusing food. It's tacky and just about making money — that's how far the whole thing has gone.'

O'Rawe's book *Blanketmen* (first published in 2005) is still to this day causing major controversy throughout the republican community long after the 25th anniversary commemorations. And O'Rawe is still standing by allegations first made in his book that the IRA's external leadership vetoed a British offer to meet most of the prisoners' demands in early July that could have saved the other six hunger strikers from death.

O'Rawe's claims have been strongly denied by leading Sinn Féin figures but backed up by former Derry priest Denis Bradley, whose long standing 'Link' comprising of himself and members of the British Security Services helped bring the IRA towards the 1994 ceasefire. Bradley said that as far as he was aware Margaret Thatcher had approved the offer O'Rawe is adamant was on the table back in 1981.

Predictably, O'Rawe has faced isolation and character assassination in his native west Belfast for daring to step out of the tribe and speak some bitter home truths about the hunger strike.

Meanwhile, the Noraid branch behind the commemorative plates, the New Jersey based Luke Dillon Unit, actually defended their decision to bring them out. The plates were being sold on www.abbyroseinc.com, an American website mainly dedicated to the sale of gravestones and monuments in New Jersey. Frank Connell of the Noraid Luke Dillon Unit and originally from Co. Cavan, said: 'Of course it's appropriate. No food after all will ever be eaten off those plates. They are purely for commemorative purposes.'

He said they intended shipping the plates not only across the United States but also to Ireland. 'We have made about 400 so far and the money raised will go to Irish Northern Aid. We hope some of them will be sold in Ireland.'

In a way who could actually blame this New Jersey Noraid chapter for bringing out this kind of tasteless kitsch? After all, the entire 25th anniversary of the hunger strike had been reduced to a series of pageants, the visages of the prisoners turned into corporate logos to sell the Sinn Féin product.

Yet the 25th anniversary of the hunger strike did at least produce some internal soul searching within the disparate Irish republican family rather than turning the entire enterprise into an unchallenged propaganda boost for Sinn Féin.

Bobby Sands's family boycotted the Sinn Féin organised commemoration inside the Maze to mark the first IRA hunger striker's death. Indeed they have tried unsuccessfully through the courts to shut down the Bobby Sands Trust and have distanced themselves from the majority of set-piece acts of remembrance Sinn Féin were behind. The Sands's hostility to the official ceremonies were and are an indication of how far the original goals that the hunger strikers went to jail for in the first place are at variance with realpolitik at Stormont today. However, this hasn't discouraged those who seek to bend and twist history in the interests of camouflaging the outcome of the Provisionals' project.

The 'laughing children' made an appearance in a Sinn Féin youth publication called *Awaiting the Lark*, released in time for the 25th anniversary. It included reminiscences from republican women like one Jennifer McCann who was twenty-one at the time of the hunger strikes. Her recollection of what it was all about was and is extremely telling:

> 'My children often asked me about the Hunger Strikers when their posters went up in the 20th anniversary campaign, and now that they're older and see them up again this year they are even more inquisitive. This conflict has been a long and hard one for a lot of people and I have seen a number of close friends and comrades die long before they were supposed to. It's then that I remember Bobby's famous quote: "Let our revenge be the laughter of our children." For me that's what the struggle is all about, our future generation living in a peaceful, just society where everyone is treated as equals.'

That last sentence is crucial evidence of the ideological retreat from old style republicanism and its unrealisable programme. The words 'peaceful, just society where everyone is treated as equals' would have been scorned by the young radicals like Sands and O'Hara in the 1970s. Such sentiments would have been dismissed as the wimpish dreams of soggy liberals and reformists, the wet dreams of the moderate elements of the Northern Ireland Civil Rights Movement. Now, of course, they are the buzz words in Sinn Féin's programme as the movement seeks cover for its necessary and belatedly welcome U-turn.

To coincide with the 25th anniversary, the Bobby Sands Trust (the very one Bobby Sands's closest loved ones are trying in vain to close) published a book of reflections on the

1981 death fast. Edited by Danny Morrison and published by Brandon Press, *Hunger Strike* provides an opportunity for an eclectic range of writers, musicians and politicians to muse on the implications of the 1981 hunger strike. It opens after a preface from Morrison with a contribution by Christy Moore. Ireland's most famous balladeer recalls his song 'I Will Sing' and, judging by what he says, it's clear Moore has learnt nothing over the last thirty years about the reality of the Northern Ireland Troubles.

'I will give it an airing each time I encounter those who seek to demean and trivialise the fallen men and their families,' Moore wrote. 'Those who seek to rewrite the story only steel my determination to remember: . . . When I hear revisionists and the downright liars, I will sing — for that is all I can do. Detractors find this pathetic and facile, but their sneering means nothing to me.'

Perhaps Christy Moore hasn't yet grasped the irony of his own words, particularly his use of the term 'revisionists' and his opposition to those who 'rewrite the story'. For in reality the entire nature of the 25th anniversary was to harness ten dead men to a political strategy, one that at least three of them would have wanted nothing to do with. The real 'revisionism' going on is the one that tries to make a tenuous link between the goals the hunger strikers went to jail for and the end product of the Provisionals' project in the first decade of the twenty-first century.

The singer ends his contribution with quotes from his song 'The Boys from Tamlaghtduff', which pays homage to the career of the second hunger striker to die, Francis Hughes. 'Francis fought them every day he lived and he fought them as he died,' sang Moore.

One wonders did Christy Moore ever consider that 'them' included not only British soldiers and RUC officers but also a ten-year-old girl who was decapitated by one of Francis Hughes's bombs. Her name was Lesley Gordon and she died along with her father, UDR part-time soldier William, after Hughes's unit detonated a booby-trap bomb under the family's car.

Moreover, if Christy Moore wants to encounter real 'revisionism' he only needs to take down the book he is quoted in from his shelf. Some of the other contributions are revealing in terms of the new revisionism necessary to defend current Sinn Féin policy. Irish-American writer Timothy O'Grady, for instance, attempted to link the hunger strike to the Good Friday Agreement seventeen years later. He reckons that all the things that occurred in the recent past pre and post the Good Friday Accord 'are the direct consequences of the dying hunger strikers placing themselves before the electorate and winning. They acted, as Gerry Adams said, in the service not of death but of life.'

Then O'Grady goes on: 'They bested the British, defeated oblivion, awakened a whole generation, but also contributed to a global movement for the human rights of prisoners and the families of the disappeared.' (Yes you heard that one right — 'the families of the disappeared.') O'Grady even mentions Chile, Argentina and Uruguay without noting that the only organisation to 'disappear' its victims during the Northern Ireland Troubles was the Provisional IRA, whose second in command in Belfast at the time of Jean McConville's disappearance was Gerry Adams. One wonders if Timothy O'Grady has even heard of Jean and the other 'disappeared' of Ireland?

The re-shaping of the hunger strike into some necessary

presage towards politicisation and ultimately historic compromise is also taken up by an old friend of Adams and co. — Tony Benn. In his contribution to *Hunger Strike*, Benn confidently asserts: 'But Bobby Sand's cause has prospered and will succeed because peace and justice are what people need and want.'

It might be worth reminding Benn that Bobby Sands and his comrades never joined the Provisional IRA to fight for ethereal notions of peace and justice. Just ask some of the closest members of his family: according to them he actually fought and died for a United Ireland.

In the course of his reflections on the hunger strike Benn also makes reference to the 2005 murder of Robert McCartney by a local IRA gang from south and east Belfast, but the British Labour left veteran fails to make any connection between the Short Strand man's killers and the Provisionals. Benn refers to 'the brutal murder of Robert McCartney by individuals' and he contends that this act of butchery was part of 'every excuse for delaying the implementation of what was promised on Good Friday'.

For Tony Benn's benefit and those who read *Hunger Strike*, these 'individuals' included Sinn Féin election workers, bodyguards to senior republican leaders and a member of the IRA's Northern Command, all of whom used the organisation's expertise to forensically cover up the killing and threaten witnesses. So the former Labour Energy Minister and one-time advocate of UN troops for Northern Ireland has not only re-written the history of the 1981 death fast for the benefit of the Adams/McGuinness project but also distorted a fundamental truth about the slaughter of Robert McCartney nearly a quarter of a century later, by claiming that somehow the IRA had absolutely nothing to do with the murder.

Hunger Strike of course contained no dissenting voices from those inside republicanism critical of the current party line. Those few that emerged from the PIRA itself to criticise the direction of the movement from the early 1990s on have been isolated and demonised within their own communities. Ex-IRA life prisoner turned academic and author Anthony McIntyre was subjected to a campaign of personal vilification in 1999 following the PIRA murder of Real IRA member Joe O'Connor. McIntyre had the audacity to speak the truth about the killing, namely that the Provisionals carried it out. His former home, where he lived with his American partner Carrie Twomey and their first child, was picketed by a baying mob. He was falsely portrayed as an ally of the Real IRA even though McIntyre has been savage in his criticism of dissident republican violence. Others such as Richard O'Rawe have also been cast into the wilderness, a kind of internal political exile where even some former comrades from the H-Blocks either won't talk to him, or won't dare be seen talking to him.

Yet no matter how effectively the Provisionals' leadership can shut down debate in their own redoubts, the outcome of the move into politics will continue to throw up awkward questions for the future.

While the electoral harvest the Provisionals reaped following the 1981 hunger strike undoubtedly convinced the majority of the republican movement about the efficacy of politics, the strategic objective remained the same: electoral politics was still only a stepping stone towards the final goal — Brits Out. Even as late as May 1991 those in the tribe most faithful to Adams emphasised that the sacrifices in the H-Blocks were part of a broader battle towards reunification and state power.

Delivering the opening address at the Bobby Sands Memorial Lecture in west Belfast that year, Jake Jackson, an Adams ally and future executive at the Andersonstown News Group, told the gathering:

'The smashing of the criminalisation policy and the broadening of the republican base which came with it marked the beginning of the end of British rule in Ireland.'

Back then there was little emphasis on laughing children or airy notions such as parity of esteem, peace or justice or indeed level playing fields. The stress was still very much that the hunger strike and the subsequent electoralism that flowed from it were all component parts of the necessary 'war'. How then to explain the journey from this die-hard radicalism to the politics of compromise?

One of the keys to answer the above question is to examine a tale of two manifestos, separated in time by almost a quarter of a century but which indicate how far the Provisionals travelled from the aftermath of the hunger strike to the present.

Within a year of the hunger strike ending, Gerry Adams engineered Sinn Féin towards its first major electoral contest — the ill-fated Assembly based on the then Northern Ireland Secretary Jim Prior's plan for 'rolling devolution'. But the party's election leaflet for west Belfast made it clear what the contest was really all about:

'BRITS OUT! SEIN FÉIN IN!' it read at the bottom of the handbill. The message was accompanied throughout the campaign with other uncompromising slogans such as proclaiming Sinn Féin to be 'The Voice of Principled Leadership' (a clear swipe at the SDLP) and of course 'Smash Stormont'. The latter imperative was marked out by a clever arrangement of Sinn Féin posters on a factory wall facing the bottom of Belfast's New Lodge Road so no one could be under any illusion — there would be no return by any nationalist, let alone republican, to the big house on the hill far away in the unionist-dominated east.

Yet there were hints, future echoes perhaps, of the kind of flexibility and pragmatism that marked Adams's later policies. On the West Belfast leaflet the party explained why it was standing in an Assembly election: 'While working for the abolition of the system, Sinn Féin believes that working people should organise to wrest as many gains from the system as possible.'

Here was a clear and early indication that the Adams-led group was ditching the destructive revolutionism of the 1970s for something more gradualist in approach.

The hard-line slogan about 'Smashing Stormont' spelt out in the green, white and orange posters along North Queen Street would not have been missed by the Provisionals' old enemies in the New Lodge, the Officials — now fully transformed into the Workers Party. Indeed the rallying cry to destroy Stormont was just across the road from the Workers Party's then base, a social club on the site of an old army barracks adjacent to Artillery House flats. It had also acted as the local headquarters of Workers Party councillor and Northern leader Seamus Lynch up until he lost his seat in the 1981 local government 'hunger strike' elections.

At the same time as the Provos were dipping their toes

into the North's electoral waters, Lynch and his party were launching a manifesto they hoped (in vain) would carry them into a new Assembly. From the 20/20 hindsight of more than three decades, the fascinating thing about the Workers Party 1982 Assembly election manifesto is that it contained many of the later demands laid down by Sinn Féin as a price for eventually entering into a Stormont parliament twenty-seven years later.

One of the cornerstones of the Workers Party manifesto was the concept of a 'Voluntary Coalition'. This would be different from the Coalition that eventually took full devolved powers in 2007 in that it wasn't mandatory.

Addressing age old and justifiable fears of a re-run of Unionist one-party misrule, the Workers Party was 'convinced that no one party will return sufficient members to the new Assembly to form a government. The alternative we envisage is the creation of a Voluntary Coalition of left and centre parties or sections of parties. Such a Coalition would produce a minimum programme of democratic, social and economic proposals and develop the Assembly as a dependable, hard working forum, committed in the interests of the vast majority in Northern Ireland, the working people.'

Leaving aside the leftist utopianism, the fanciful notion that there was such a thing as a potentially strong left and centrist bloc in the Assembly in the first place, it is worth noting that the Workers Party's call for checks and balances — aimed at restraining the potential for one-party misrule — were the same ones sought by Sinn Féin even before Good Friday 1998, again as the price for entering what was still a partitionist parliament. And although the agreements hammered out during Easter week 1998 and latterly at St Andrews in the autumn of 2006 resulted in a forced marriage of the parties, the broad framework envisaged by Sinn Féin's old street foes was and is largely the same.

Other political demands contained in the Workers Party manifesto are also precursors to what were to become 'confidence building measures' for the Provisionals throughout the peace process. In a section of the Workers Party paper entitled 'No Progress without peace', for instance, the party calls for the repeal of all emergency laws and the end of the British army's primary role in security. Moreover, the party lambastes the 'abuses by state forces', which they claimed 'drive our society down a backward and reactionary path'.

Movement out of this cul de sac, the Workers Party envisaged, would be enabled by policing reforms. On the issue of the police, the party confidently stated that the 'ordinary man and woman is crying out for a total de-militarisation of society . . . end the use of plastic baton rounds' etc; these were all to become critical Sinn Féin demands decades later. Indeed de-militarisation in areas such as South Armagh was seen as critical to winning over the republican base beyond the redoubts intensely loyal to Gerry Adams towards the new peaceful way forward.

Another product of the peace process and Good Friday Agreement was the creation of the office of the Police Ombudsman. Again, back in 1982 the Workers Party was arguing for such a post.

'The Workers Party therefore calls for the establishment of a totally independent body to be charged with investigating complaints against the police, having the power to present evidence and make recommendations to the Chief Constable and the DPP.'

There is also a precursory demand for a Policing Board: 'We demand that it should be democratised by representation from the Assembly, from the trade unions, from civil liberties, tenant organisations etc.' (Interestingly the one social movement with thousands of members on both sides of the sectarian divide, operating on an all island basis — the trade union movement — remains the only force still unrepresented on the North's current Policing Board.)

The 1982 Assembly election marked the first serious attempt by the Official republicans, now the Workers Party, to build an electoral base across the divide and start garnering votes from the Northern Protestant community. Their efforts were, of course, derided by the Provisionals and their sympathisers on the far left. The results of the election, which left the party with no Assembly seats, was surely evidence, their critics argued, of the futility of trying to reach out to such a reactionary bloc as the unionists. But then fast forward through twenty-one years to the 2003 Assembly elections and the message Sinn Féin is now transmitting to that same politico-religious bloc, the unionists, is not all that dissimilar to the one the Workers Party tried in vain to communicate just less than twelve months after the hunger strike.

Sinn Féin's 2003 manifesto was a glossy production, with Gerry Adams now in a suit as opposed to the white polo neck and anorak we saw on the 1982 'Brits Out, Sinn Féin In', leaflet.

The most significant section of the manifesto is on page 22, entitled 'Engaging with unionists'. After detailing Alex Maskey's outreach as Belfast Lord Mayor to all communities in the city, the party notes that 'We are individually and together going through a period of change in our society. It is important that unionism joins with the rest of us in managing that process.'

There is still the United Ireland imperative, although less strident and uncompromising than in the past: 'Whilst nationalists, republicans and unionists are engaging in a process of change, so too must society change to accommodate all of us who live on the island. A united Ireland must be inclusive for all and must guarantee the rights and entitlements of unionists so that they have a sense of security and a state in the new Ireland.'

This reach-out-to-unionists love-bombing is all a far cry from the rage and anger of the 1982 leaflet, where the author blamed all of west Belfast's ills on the 'worst excesses of its [the British] administration' and of course 'unionist domination'. And all a far cry too from the anti-Colonist rhetoric of the 1980s and all those soft *Magill* interviews.

There are past echoes too in the slickly produced Sinn Féin document especially on policing which remind one of the old Workers Party manifesto. The key demands are a need for a demilitarised PSNI; the end of plastic bullets and democratic control of policing. There is even talk of a Constitutional Court, the expansion of the role of the Human Rights Commission and of course that old Workers Party demand for a Bill of Rights. Indeed some of the language is remarkably similar to the Workers Party's at the time of Jim Prior's devolution project.

'Given the effect of 30 years of conflict, a strong bill of rights is required to provide citizens, especially those most vulnerable of our society, with the means to avail of their rights . . . In our wide ranging submissions to the Human Rights Commission SF called for a comprehensive Bill of Rights for the North as a first step towards the fullest harmonisations of rights standards throughout the island.'

Overall there are eighteen chapters or sections in the manifesto, seven of which deal with contentious issues ranging from praise for the IRA in the peace process to an old Workers Party-style demand for a Bill of Rights. From pages 8 to 15 the party deals with bread and butter issues, although the odd piece of green leaf is chucked in to create the impression of an all Ireland sandwich.

The manifesto is prefaced with a letter from Adams which is couched in the language of the SDLP. There is no mention in his epistle of a democratic, socialist republic anymore. The S-word too is completely absent. It even argues on page 48 that the 'Six Counties' should 'develop and target tax incentives towards areas of high unemployment'.

In Adams's letter, 'equality' or the 'struggle against inequality' is mentioned at least six times, all-Ireland is mentioned twice, while new Ireland is stated once. The manifesto also talks about 'Tackling the British Treasury'. Not so much putting that Treasury out of business but rather developing 'a new mechanism for calculating the Block Grant . . .' That is the block grant from the British Treasury.

Quite troubling perhaps for Thomas 'Slab' Murphy and his South Armagh Brigade the party also calls on page 13 (unlucky for some?) for the 'harmonisation of Irish fuel taxes', which would undoubtedly mean an end to cheap washed smuggled diesel into Northern Ireland, and an end to the South Armagh smugglers' business.

Finally there was a telling image on page 11 which

introduces the section 'Building an Ireland of Equals'. It is of MPs Michelle Gildernew and Pat Doherty and it had been taken outside the entrance to the British House of Commons. Such a vista in a Sinn Féin manifesto would have been impossible to envisage even just a few years earlier.

There is one fundamental contrast between this tale of two manifestos and it is the domination of one figure in the latter. The 2003 election booklet is shot through with the Gerry Adams personality cult. Out of forty-six images in the manifesto there are at least seventeen of the party president, reflecting the absolutely critical role he played and continues to play in Sinn Féin's electoral advances. In reality his ubiquitous presence throughout the election literature also underlines how tightly he controlled the reins of power in the movement.

Combining the cult of the personality and the deployment of 'future generations' (the laughing children), as well as all the dead ones of course, the movement maintained a sense of purpose, unity and direction through pageantry. Active Service Units became local commemoration societies, with members raising finance for the construction of memorials to fallen comrades and organising pilgrimages to these sites.

Although armed republicanism had always paid homage to the fallen from other 'struggles', from 1798 onwards, in the twelve years from the 1994 ceasefire these acts of commemoration intensified on an industrial scale. In part this was the transmission of a message, a monthly, often weekly, act of communication to claim that they had not sold out the martyred dead, as if the act of remembrance almost alone could obscure the new road the movement was undertaking. In addition, it maintained a sense of comrade-ship and togetherness as the old boys met and marched as one and talked about old times after their parades.

A similar process was also taking place within the loyalist paramilitary groups. Memorials and dedication-days in loyalist areas never looked as pristine and disciplined, compared to the time of the Troubles. In the UVF's case, after their ceasefire the movement adopted the fashion of World War One militaria. UVF bands formed up decked out in the uniforms of the Great War; brand new murals were painted depicting scenes from the Battle of the Somme; even plays were put on based on Ulster working-class characters living out the horrors of trench warfare. A huge amount of resources and time were spent not only in commemorating the UVF dead but also reaching back into history, trying to connect up their terror 'war' just past with the global struggles of the twentieth century. (To many in Northern Ireland and beyond who had ancestors that actually fought in battles like the Somme, the idea of comparing enlisted men, the fallen of trench warfare, with masked paramilitaries who more often than not shot their victims and ran off was an obscene parallel.) Overall, however, on both sides there was something in common: at least the 'boys' were being kept busy.

This unique brand of Irish/Ulster memorialism brings to mind the poetic insight of the English writer and journalist James Fenton when, during a long tenure in Berlin, he confronted a generation of Germans who dedicated the remainder of their lives to burying the past. In his poem 'German Requiem', Fenton wrote: 'How comforting it is, once or twice a year, to get together and forget the old times.'

But the 'boys of the not so old brigade' who still meet 'once or twice a year' at memorial sites all over the North of Ireland cannot be accused of forgetting old times. Rather they commemorate as a means to re-shape the past and in turn distort the present.

This has been going on even prior to the ceasefires in the nascent period of the peace process or Hume-Adams talks. It is a phenomenon that even stretches back to the Spanish Civil War and the contribution of Belfast republicans and leftists in the struggle to defend the Spanish Republic against Franco's fascist forces. In the early 1990s there was an exhibition on the Spanish Civil War held at Conway Mill off the Falls Road, a community centre with strong ties to Sinn Féin and the republican movement. The exhibits included photographs from key battles and a roll of honour dedicated to the men who fought for the Spanish Republic from Belfast and all across Ireland. One man though was missing from the list — Paddy McAllister. He lived just a couple of hundred yards away from where the exhibition took place in the Lower Falls. McAllister was in fact the only surviving Spanish Civil War veteran who fought for the Spanish Republic still living in west Belfast. Yet he was neither invited to the event nor was his contribution mentioned in it. The reason for erasing this then walking and breathing old soldier for the Spanish Republican cause was that he had the 'wrong' political allegiance. In the 1969–70 split McAllister sided with the Officials and remained loyal to them right up until his death. For that reason alone he was airbrushed out of the commemoration.

The PIRA's equivalent of the UVF's historical/militaristic post-ceasefire pageantry reached its climax on New Year's

Day 2007. Dressed in 1950s style IRA uniforms, carrying real but now de-activated Lee Enfield rifles and Sten sub-machine-guns, a lorry load of 'volunteers' crossed the border from the Republic into Fermanagh. They were re-enacting the raid on Brookeborough RUC station exactly fifty years earlier in which Fergal O'Hanlon and Sean South died. Ironically perhaps, the only prominent living survivor of that raid back in 1957, who was himself badly wounded in the exchange of gunfire with besieged RUC officers trapped in the station, was Sean Garland, now President of the Workers Party. He didn't get an invitation. Not that he would have wanted one. Garland was a long and bitter opponent of the Provisionals throughout the Troubles. Moreover, at the time any fresh excursion North across the border by Garland could have resulted in his arrest, not for the raid on Brookeborough but rather to face accusations that he had masterminded a sophisticated international dollar-forgery operation with the help of the North Korean regime.

Instead, the re-run of the Brookeborough raid was a chance for Gerry Adams, the main guest speaker, to again underscore the supposed unbroken connection between the police station raiders of Operation Harvest and modern day Sinn Féin, which ironically was just about to sign up to support the PSNI.

Not only did mainstream republicans dress up to replay past set piece events in Irish history, they also 'dressed up' the nature of their 'war'. This was done during the violence to morally defend the sabotage and the assassinations. Thus, for instance, Danny Morrison, while Sinn Féin Publicity Director, drew parallels between the IRA and the Maquis or French Resistance of World War Two. Murals too made comparisons between the Nazi treatment of Jews, Gypsies and any political opponents, and the British treatment of nationalists and republicans in Northern Ireland. These absurd and insidious parallels were not Sinn Féin copyright alone; they seeped into broader Northern nationalist/ Catholic consciousness and even coloured literature. The highly under-rated Belfast-born poet Padraig Fiacc, for instance, once dared to compare the plight of Catholics under sectarian threat from loyalists to the Jews in Nazi Germany in one of his poems contained inside his brilliantly terrifying collection *Odour of Blood*.

But pre and post the ceasefires it was the Provisionals who most regularly deployed the Nazi parallel. One mural painted to record the controversial and disgraceful killing of a young man from the nationalist Lower Ormeau Road at the start of the 1980s illustrated this. This painting on a wall in a street leading to the Beechmount area of west Belfast depicted the police officer shooting the teenager on the Lower Ormeau Road. However, beside the recreation of this incident were pictorial references to Buchenwald Concentration Camp along with a figure dressed in a black Gestapo uniform cracking a whip. The Maze prison also became transformed somehow into Auschwitz and Dachau. During the 1981 hunger strike the supporters and demonstrators chanted: 'H-Block, H-Block, you named it well. H for Hitler and H for hell.'

The double irony of the Nazi parallels is that present-day republicans still revere IRA leaders who were allied to Nazi Germany in the Second World War. They still gather every September to honour Sean Russell at a statue of the IRA commander during World War Two in Dublin's Fairview

Park. Among those who have in recent years addressed the annual Sean Russell memorial service is Mary Lou McDonald, Sinn Féin's MEP for Dublin. It is ironic that a member of the United Left group in the European Parliament was honouring an ally of the Nazis who died on a German submarine on route back to Ireland to foment a terror campaign aimed at undermining Britain's and the Allies' war effort. Like Paddy McAllister from the left, Sean Russell's alignment with the Nazis has been conveniently sidelined to the margins of republican history.

Yet even after the last IRA 'war' was long over, republicans continued to draw parallels with Nazi Germany. In the Christmas 2006 edition of the republican youth magazine *Awaiting the Lark*, Gerry Adams's brother Dominic got carried away on a visit to former Nazi concentration camps that summer. In his report for the magazine, he made a libellous parallel between Long Kesh/Maze and the Sachsenhausen and Breedock concentration camps, respectively in Berlin and Belgium. Dominic Adams wrote that he was impressed that Breedock is one of 'the best conserved camps in Europe' and a model for the way the Maze should be preserved as a museum.

As well as the offensive kitsch-comparisons to the Nazi death camps, the propagandists of the 'armed struggle' also equated the actions of the British state with dictatorships. In the same British-state-funded community magazine, for instance, one writer from South Armagh, James Long, took a swipe at 'self styled human rights organisations throughout the world'. In his tirade Long mentioned China and predicted an onslaught of complaints about the regime's human rights record before and during the 2008 Olympic Games.

He wrote: 'No doubt this human rights argument will carry on up to and beyond the Beijing games in China in 2008.' Tired of hearing about human rights groups, Long wondered 'will we witness the same exposé of British government human rights abuses — I fear not.'

The above stands alone as a classic piece of uber kitsch-comparison, the burning desire to see your plight painted in the darkening light of far worse political and social situations. For a start, many of these 'self styled human rights organisations', such as Amnesty International, have in fact highlighted and severely criticised British state abuses in Northern Ireland down through the decades. They were never silent. More offensive still is the attempt to equate these British state abuses — Internment, Castlereagh beatings, individual acts of collusion etc. — with a regime which, since it took power at the end of the 1940s, has been responsible for the deaths of millions upon millions of its own citizens through state-induced famine, terrorisation and mass fanaticism.

For now at least the laughing children have so far drowned out the muted cries of sell-out and surrender from the republican dissident rump, most of which only offers the nihilism of continued 'armed struggle' and its inevitable final stop — prison or an early grave.

But perhaps the most astonishing achievement of the Adams peace strategy has been the ability to persuade not only a majority of the republican base but large sections of Sinn Féin's new electorate that the Provisionals have not gone down the 'sticky road' of compromise and accommodation with unionism. Which of course is exactly the route they have followed.

At the end of the twentieth century, IRA prisoners were taking stock of the decade between 1989 and 1999. In *Coiste na n-Iarchimi: Political Issues in Ireland*, Volume 1, there was a series of articles by republican prisoners, some named, some un-named. The early articles are instructive in measuring how far the leadership was to travel from revolutionary romanticism to realism. One of the earliest, written by an anonymous prisoner in the autumn of 1989, dealt with mainstream republicanism's attitude to the Irish Republic. There is one key sentence that summed up Northern republicans' alienation from the Southern political entity: 'The independence of 1922 for the "Free State" has proven illusory — the economy has been dominated by British finance and multinational capital and its interests.'

Less than twenty years later Gerry Adams was, during the 2007 Irish general election, holding up the Celtic Tiger economy — the most neo-liberal, Anglo-Saxon Atlanticist economic model in Western Europe — as a success story and, more critically still, as a rational economic justification for unionists to join the Republic.

Possibly the twenty-first century Adams is right in that one regard — the prosperity of the hyper-capitalist Republic of Ireland may eventually woo a significant segment of hard-headed business-minded unionists away from the UK. The union therefore may not ultimately be broken by the rising of the Men of No Property, as Wolfe Tone and later the republican civil war die-hard Liam Mellows once envisaged, but rather the Men and Women of rising House Price Property Values. And speaking of property, many senior figures in Sinn Féin, not just Adams himself with his holiday home in Donegal, but other leading activists are now substantially wealthy individuals, much of their new prosperity derived from investments in second homes, businesses, land and, in the case of one former Belfast IRA commander, ownership of substantial tracts of Divis Mountain!

But even if that remote scenario eventually unfolds, the final outcome of the 'struggle' is unlikely to deliver the kind of final result Adams and all the other former social republicans and leftists once dreamed about during the years of fusing 'armed struggle' and 'people's politics'. No amount of laughing children can distract from that reality.

Yet the collective self-delusion alongside the kitch-comparisons continued into 2008, even as more informants within the movement were being exposed. The 7 February edition of *An Phoblacht/Republican News* reported the creation of yet another think-tank, one which spanned the border and incorporated the nine counties of the ancient province of Ulster. 'Cuige Uladh' held its first AGM in Letterkenny and guest speaker was the party President. One of the keynote speakers was the man regarded as one of the party's most important behind-the-scenes strategists, the Queen's University graduate and Sinn Féin strategist Declan Kearney.

Mindful that 2008 marked the 40th anniversary of the Vietnamese National Liberation Front's Tet Offensive against American occupation, Kearney cheered up the comrades with some lessons from the achievements of Ho Chi Minh's army.

The *An Phoblacht/Republican News* writer noted that Kearney used the experience of the Vietnam War and the Tet

Offensive to 'draw some crucial analogies with the struggle in Ireland'. Kearney reminded the gathering that the Americans lost the initiative, never to regain it after the 1968 offensive. Somehow he managed to bend and twist logic to argue that the DUP's decision to enter government with Sinn Féin had been a deft political manoeuvre reminiscent of the NLF's master-stroke at Tet. And just as the NLF/Viet Cong had targeted South Vietnam, so the Provisionals must zero in on Southern Ireland.

'The battle for unity will be won or lost in the 26 Counties. We need to understand that when we talk about the strategic battle lines having shifted South,' he predicted, before referring to Sinn Féin losses in the 2007 Irish general election.

> 'Last May's election demonstrated the strength of the political forces arraigned against us. The political establishment in the 26 Counties is out to crush our struggle so we need to get our defences in order. That means we must build our organisation across the 26 Counties.
>
> We need to get back the momentum in the South, we need to build the party, we need to get on with the work of campaigning around issues that make a real difference to people's lives.
>
> If we don't regain the momentum in the South, our project will be holed below the waterline.
>
> Tet required a beach-head in North Vietnam. Ulster has to be the beachhead from which we launch our offensive into the South.'

But such is the ideological suppleness of the Provisionals that at the very same conference Gerry Adams was able deftly to move from Ho Chi Minh to Milton Friedman. In his address Adams again returned to the theme of Irish business.

'We are pro-business. Neither are we a high-tax party although we are against the "super profits" being made by the multi-nationals and the big banks, like the obscene $31.3 billion profit announced this week by Shell.'

Despite the reference to Shell (an easy 'foreign' target to keep the radicals and leftists happy), Adams's remarks again underlined that the party was embracing the market economy, in just the same way as the successors of the NLF did post-1989 back in Vietnam. Whether or not Adams's injunction that Sinn Féin was not anti-business was a put-down to the party's radical chic wing, the implication was clear — Sinn Féin wouldn't be marching down the cul de sac of ultra-left protest. Those few remaining in Sinn Féin with pretensions to Marxist-Leninist doctrine would go the same way that earlier leftist hangers-on such as the PD exiles had gone — straight into the political wilderness. The disjunction meantime between Declan Kearney's Vietcong/NLF analogy and Sinn Féin's realism was as glaring as ever. Because while the secretary of 'Cuige Uladh' waxed lyrical about the example of the NLF's most famous military operation, Gerry Adams's key ally in the United States remained a conservative Republican, Peter King, who himself was allied to the Vietcong's most famous former prisoner-of-war, Naval pilot John McCain, currently in the race for the US Presidency!

The ludicrous parallels drawn by Kearney between Sinn Féin's push for more votes in the Irish Republic and the Tet uprising forty years earlier were made all the more absurd within days of that edition of *An Phoblacht/Republican News* hitting the streets. On the morning of 8 February rumours were circulating about another long-term British spy operating within the IRA's ranks in Belfast. In the early hours of that morning agents from MI5 knocked on the door of Roy McShane's Lower Falls home in west Belfast. They had a grim warning for him: he was about to be outed as an informer and would in all likelihood eventually suffer the same fate as Sinn Féin's Chief of Administration at Stormont, Denis Donaldson: someone would assassinate him.

The 58-year-old was firstly taken to MI5's gleaming new headquarters at Holywood outside Belfast before being flown by British army helicopter across the Irish Sea and into protective custody in Britain. Before leaving the new intelligence services' HQ (whose location was part of the St Andrews Agreement signed up to by among others Sinn Féin), McShane was allowed to telephone his family and confess his sins.

From the outset Sinn Féin desperately tried to play down the importance of McShane's betrayal. They insisted he was not party to any major negotiations and had never held a senior role within the republican movement in Belfast. However, McShane had been one of Gerry Adams's chauffeurs from the early 1990s, part of a pool of drivers and security officers drawn from the IRA's ranks. He had also ferried other republican leaders such as Martin McGuinness to key meetings. McShane clearly had access to the top echelons of mainstream republicanism. The driving pool was regarded as one of the most trusted units in the organisation. At one time it had been headed up by Terence 'Cleeky'

Clarke, one of the Provisionals' leading figures in Ardoyne and up until his death a close confidant and friend of Adams's.

In addition, McShane hadn't always been just a mere wheel-man for senior Sinn Féin and IRA figures. Ironically he had been part of the IRA's 'nutting squad' in the 1980s, the Provisionals' internal security unit that sought out and killed informers inside the movement. The unmasking of McShane as an informer was yet further evidence that one of the most secretive, ruthless and important units of the IRA was deeply compromised. After all, McShane's boss in the 'nutting squad' or 'head hunters' was none other than Freddie Scappaticci, AKA Stake Knife, one of Britain's most important agents inside the Provisionals. The revelation that yet another IRA 'head hunter' was a paid agent of the British state again raises questions about the morality of running informers involved in serious crimes up to and, certainly in Stake Knife's case, including murder. In a further irony, old comrades later recalled that when Denis Donaldson had been exposed as a British agent, McShane had been one of the most vocal among those in favour of calling for Sinn Féin's Chief of Administration at Stormont to be 'executed'!

Moreover, McShane at one time commanded the IRA's unit in the Turf Lodge district and had been involved in republicanism even prior to the 1969–70 split. At one time he had even shared a house with the future Official IRA leader in the city, Billy McMillen. Old comrades of McMillen (who was shot dead by a sixteen-year-old INLA gunman in a feud in the mid-1970s) now believe McShane may have been a long-term pre-split plant within the Provisionals, although a number of PIRA sources insist he was recruited much later, possibly after being blackmailed over sexual proclivities. Whatever the origins of McShane's treachery, what this all indicates is that the various branches of the British security forces had a bewildering range of informers and agents of influence operating inside both the IRA and Sinn Féin. In 'England's Vietnam', therefore, pace the kitsch-fantasies of Declan Kearney and the other faithful attending Cuige Uladh's AGM, if there had been an 'Irish Tet' offensive then it would, given the level of British security penetration, be more likely to have been run by General Westmoreland rather than Ho Chi Minh, General Giap or any of the other NLF commanders.

Just a few weeks after the exposé of McShane, another IRA icon from the 1970s passed away. In the latter stages of his life Brendan 'Darkie' Hughes had been one of the sharpest critics of Sinn Féin's direction and in particular the leadership of his old comrade Gerry Adams. Hughes had led the IRA's most adept unit in the early 1970s and scored some considerable coups against the British army, including running a unit that had broken into the British military's communication system at Thiepval Barracks, Lisburn. The Lower Falls republican veteran had later been captured in leafy south Belfast posing as a middle-class businessmen, perfect cover for the most important IRA unit in the city at the time. Later he led the first IRA hunger strike in 1980 aimed at restoring political status for republican prisoners in Long Kesh/Maze jail. Articulate in front of the camera (even as a gaunt, bearded, defiant hunger striker on the cusp of death) and a fearless and dedicated street fighter, Hughes could have been one of the leading figures in the movement after he emerged from prison having served thirteen years in jail. However, he went back to a life of labouring, working on west Belfast building sites, even organising a strike because of the poor pay and conditions, an action which angered the IRA leadership due to their financial links with the contractor.

Although Hughes had opposed the Good Friday Agreement — dubbing it 'Got F*** All' — the 59-year-old never advocated a return to 'war'. Indeed a year after the Agreement was signed, when the PIRA shot dead Real IRA member from Ballymurphy Joe O'Connor, Hughes implored republican dissidents in west Belfast not to strike back and thus launch a major feud with the Provisionals. The dissidents had come to Hughes directly after the O'Connor funeral in 1999 to ask for his advice. The only counsel he offered them was that violence was not the proper response. This was an important moment and signalled perhaps that Hughes had already concluded that the 'war' had been entirely futile.

Later, in an interview with the author, Hughes acknowledged that if he had ever imagined the outcome of the struggle would be a power-sharing executive at Stormont, with Sinn Féin sitting down alongside unionists in a devolved parliament still under final UK sovereign control, then he never would have signed up for 'war' in the first place. Coming from the lips of someone who sacrificed so much in his own life (he had for example lost his wife through years of imprisonment), it was an astonishing admission. Here was one of the IRA's most renowned and respected 'soldiers' questioning whether it had all been worth it. The obvious answer is, of course, that it wasn't, ever, even if Hughes couldn't admit it in public.

Brendan Hughes drank himself to death, alcohol becoming a daily palliative for the personal anguish he suffered, brought on by a life, in its latter stages, of deep disillusionment. He ended his days alone in his apartment in Divis Tower, which his friends later claimed had been bugged on the orders of the IRA leadership.

But even in death Hughes could not escape the strategems of those he fundamentally believed had abandoned purist republicanism. Shortly before he died of massive organ failure, Sinn Féin's slick PR machine fed stories to the media in Belfast that Hughes had sent for his old comrade Gerry Adams. There were whispers that they had reached some sort of a rapprochement, that Hughes had sought to mend fences with Adams and atone for his withering criticism of the Sinn Féin President over the last decade. After the reports of Adams holding Hughes's hand on his deathbed came the funeral in the Lower Falls. There have been conflicting accounts too of the events surrounding 23 February 2008, with claims flying from all the various factions of dissident republicanism that Sinn Féin and in particular Adams 'hijacked' the funeral. Marion Price and Anthony McIntyre openly accused Adams of elbowing priests and mourners alike out of the way to get to the front of the cortège and in line of sight of news media cameras. If this had been the Sinn Féin chief's true intention then it clearly worked. A generally compliant and gullible Northern Ireland media led their reports on the Hughes funeral with the angle of Adams carrying the coffin and his deathbed visitation earlier that week to his old Long Kesh Cage 11 comrade. In the main the media failed to mention how alienated Hughes had been in his later years from Adams in particular.

A few veteran correspondents from the UK did, however, conclude that Sinn Féin had staged yet another daring PR coup, seizing control of the publicity surrounding the funeral of one of their potentially most dangerous republican critics. West Belfast's President of Forgetting had brilliantly managed a set-piece republican event — the volunteer's funeral — and prevented it from becoming a rally point against his leadership, against his strategy. He was also blessed with good fortune. Adams's old rival, the man who had been court-marshalled back in the 1980s for attempting to overthrow the West Belfast MP's leadership, Ivor Malachy Bell, had been scheduled to give the oration at Hughes's funeral. However, forty-eight hours before Hughes's final journey, Bell had reportedly fallen ill and was unable to attend. There would therefore be no graveside last tribute, no opportunity for Bell to deliver in absentia Hughes's political will and testament.

Like the 'laughing children', Brendan Hughes in death had become a useful tool in the project to obscure past crimes and, more crucially still, cover up present compromises. No matter how much the dissidents continued to protest, the fact remained that Sinn Féin's support base would in the main believe the narrative now being dictated by Adams and his allies. One of the wayward 'Freedom's Sons' — the sobriquet the 2nd battalion of the Provisional IRA used to refer to themselves — had been brought back into Adams's fold, although Darkie Hughes, already in a coma when the Big Lad clasped his hand, knew nothing about it nor indeed had given his benediction to such a controversial rehabilitation. And given that Hughes had failed to write a memoir or make himself available for a final interview, there would be no revenge from beyond the grave.

Chapter Five

Stalking a Lost Deed

When the IRA border campaign officially ended on 27 February 1962, the republican movement had some harsh words for the Irish people. One of the reasons the IRA Army Council had decided to call off its six-year campaign of assassination and sabotage was that those they sought to liberate did not appear to be ready for it; or worse still, didn't want it.

'Foremost among the factors motivating this course of action has been the attitude of the general public whose minds have been deliberately distracted from the supreme issue facing the Irish people — the unity and freedom of Ireland,' the leadership explained. The people clearly didn't know what was good for them. But just like the Bolsheviks, this armed radical minority would continue to act on behalf of the people and when the time was right they would seize the moment. In other words, the vanguard of the national revolution would wait for another day; there would be no drawing a line under the past. In its statement the IRA warned it would be back and renewing 'its pledge of external hostility to the British forces of occupation in Ireland'.

The 'armed struggle' of 1956 to 1962 had been a costly one for the IRA, especially in terms of personnel. In its opening phase — the attack on Brookeborough RUC Station on New Year's Day 1956 — the movement had lost two volunteers, Sean South and Fergal O'Hanlon. Among the other IRA fatalities of that phase of 'struggle' was a self-inflicted blow the following year at Edentubber, Co. Louth, just a couple of miles from the South Armagh border. Five men died while transporting a bomb which was meant to have been detonated at a nearby frontier customs post.

Almost exactly fifty years after that disastrous IRA 'own goal', Gerry Adams returned to the scene in circumstances radically different from the ones that the Edentubber martyrs had lived and died under. His party was now in a power-sharing government with Ian Paisley, the price of which was Sinn Féin accepting the legitimacy of the Police Service of Northern Ireland. Indeed, from the Edentubber platform he even called for co-operation with both the Garda Síochána and the PSNI in the investigation into the recent murder of South Armagh man Paul Quinn.

At the annual commemoration for those who died in the Edentubber explosion, Adams was addressing republicans to re-affirm their commitment to a Brit-free United Ireland. Yet in addition to the usual dedications in honour of these particular fallen, Adams used the occasion on 11 November 2007 to denounce what he described as 'micro groups', meaning the Real IRA and the Continuity IRA. He also referred to the late Provo-legend Martin Meehan and how he and his family had come under pressure from these very same dissidents just before he died of a heart attack.

> 'Martin Meehan and his wife Briege received five death threats from these elements in the week before his untimely death. No republican objectives are advanced by such behaviour. On the contrary the activities of these groups play into the hands of those who are against change. These groups have no strategy, no programmes, no popular support and no real capacity — militarily or otherwise.
>
> They have chosen random acts of intimidation and isolated acts of individual violence which are politically ineffective and result only in pain and suffering for the individuals targeted and their families. The overall effect is retrograde at every level and in every sense when what is required is forward momentum. I would appeal to them once again therefore to cease all activities. I will engage with all or any of these groups to persuade them of the imperative for everyone genuinely interested in republicanism to advance it in a peaceful manner.'

Adams's denunciation came in between two separate Real IRA attacks on two police officers, one in Derry, the other in Dungannon. Which no doubt Adams would have regarded as exactly the kind of 'random acts of intimidation and isolated acts of individual violence which are politically ineffective'.

But were these modern day 'random acts' any different

really at all from those of the self-declared liberators who blew themselves up at Edentubber almost fifty years earlier? Certainly Adams's latter day biting analysis of the strategy of violence sounded remarkably similar to that advanced within the republican community under the leadership of Cathal Goulding after the end of Operation Harvest as the IRA in the Sixties sought a new way forward. The only difference, in fact, remains the timeline, the space of fifty years between one critique of the use of arms as a counter-productive policy and another in a brand new century. Only the actors had now changed, and there was also the not small matter of nearly 3,500 dead in between.

In the morally distorted world of Irish paramilitarism the dissidents have at least one thing in their favour: cold-hearted logic. Take their attempt to assassinate a Catholic PSNI officer in Derry while he was dropping off his son to school just over a week before Adams's Edentubber speech. The method of the attempted murder and the strategic motive behind it would have been familiar to many of the ageing cadres gathered around that border monument on Remembrance Sunday 2007.

Analyse the motive first. At the beginning of the Provisionals' campaign the leadership quite deliberately targeted and killed Catholic members of the RUC and the locally recruited Ulster Defence Regiment. The aim was quite obviously to deter any Catholic or nationalist from either staying in or indeed joining the British security forces. By doing so the Provisionals could portray the RUC as entirely Protestant and thus an innately unionist dominated force. Catholic police officers therefore were prime targets, branded in death as traitors to their community. For those Catholic officers that survived the Troubles, they lived their lives cut off in many cases from their wider family circles, particularly for those who came from nationalist working-class areas.

No matter how morally repugnant and revolting the notion of attempting to gun down a man who has just left his son at the school gates, the rationale (in the paramilitary universe at least) motivating the two would-be assassins on that Derry street in November 2007 was no different than the one that drove dozens of PIRA activists to target, hunt down and in many cases kill Catholic policemen and women within living memory. Only the alphabetic nomenclature of the would-be assassins had changed.

In this bizarre turn of events we need to return again to Milan Kundera and his assessment of how by the dawn of the 1960s the young idealists who followed the post-war communist ideal had begun to hunt down that which they had unleashed onto the world.

> 'And suddenly those young, intelligent radicals had the strange feeling of having sent something into the world, a deed of their making, which had taken on a life of its own, lost all resemblance to the original idea, and today ignored the originators of that idea. So those young, intelligent radicals started shouting to their deed, calling it back, scolding it, chasing it, hunting it down. If I were to write a novel about that generation of talented radical thinkers, I would call it "Stalking a Lost Deed".'

By 1968 this group of 'talented radical thinkers', even those loyal to the original goals of the Communist Manifesto, had the 'deed' firmly in their cross-hairs. The 'Prague Spring' almost witnessed the culling in one country of socialism-from-above but that was instead crushed with the influx of 5,000 Soviet tanks and the re-imposition of totalitarian rule for another twenty-one years.

For the last decade and a half (perhaps even arguably, in the case of Gerry Adams's true agenda, for the last twenty years) the present mainstream republican leadership haven't so much been 'stalking a lost deed' but rather are being both haunted and hunted by it. The thing they sent into the world refuses to recede into the mists of history, to become as irrelevant and remote as Carthage or Byzantium. And in part the 'deed's' unwillingness to leave the stage is because within living memory those they stalk once did exactly what they are now doing.

Thirty years after the 'Prague Spring' on an August afternoon in a County Tyrone market town a bomb exploded, killing twenty-nine men, women and children and wounding hundreds of others, many scarred for life. Twenty-four hours after the Omagh atrocity Martin McGuinness turned up outside the town's leisure centre, which was being used as a clearing house of information for families and loved ones trying to discover if their relatives, friends or partners had been caught up in the explosion. McGuinness's presence that Sunday morning was a vivid example of the republican leadership stalking their lost deed. The Real IRA, according to Sinn Féin's chief negotiator, was now the 'Surreal IRA'. Lining up beside the Mid Ulster MP was Sinn Féin councillor after councillor, all there to condemn the atrocity.

For some foreign reporters and commentators present on the day, McGuinness turning up there to show solidarity with the victims marked an historic tipping point. Omagh would be the last atrocity and republican leaders like McGuinness would ensure it wouldn't happen again, they concluded.

There is no doubt, judging by his demeanour and the tone of his voice, that McGuinness was visibly shocked at the bomb's aftermath. However, on that bleak Sunday morning there were two nagging thoughts exercising the minds of some of the veterans of the Ulster press corps. Many turned their minds back to similar explosions, several of them IRA 'operations', which had led to multiple civilian deaths. The Real IRA later said they had never intended to leave the car bomb where it was abandoned — right in the heart of the town's commercial centre. They had in fact planned to leave it in another spot where it would be designed to detonate as police and troops cleared the town centre following an inadequate bomb warning. Their intended targets were soldiers and policemen, or 'combatants' to use republican parlance. How many times had the IRA been forced to respond in similar fashion when bomb, mortar and mine attacks intended to be directed at the security forces killed civilians instead? The 'deed' in the shape of the Real IRA could hark back to these same 'mistakes' of the very recent past and charge their former comrades in the summer of 1998 with rank hypocrisy.

Former IRA prisoner turned writer Anthony McIntyre also noted shortly after the massacre that the entire modus operandi of the Omagh bomb (plant a device, lure in the security forces, catch them unaware as they clear the scene) had been invented by the Provisionals. The Provos had, to recall McIntyre's own words at the time, 'their intellectual fingerprints all over the Omagh bomb'. In fact, it is worth stressing again that it was the IRA which invented the car bomb all the way back in 1970.

None of the above is at all to suggest that Martin McGuinness shouldn't have turned up as Omagh was coming to terms with its terrible losses. Not only did he represent a substantial body of opinion in the North of Ireland, his decision to come to Omagh as future Education Minister represented for tens of thousands of others, even those who would never contemplate supporting Sinn Féin, a welcome development, a symbolic demonstration that at least the mainstream brand of republicanism was finally recognising the futility of the 'war' and would end it for good.

After Omagh it actually seemed that the 'deed' had indeed been cornered and was about to be slain. Even in Dundalk, a town so long synonymous with the IRA on-the-runs from the North, there was unprecedented anger. Ordinary citizens marched to the home of Michael McKevitt, the Real IRA's founder and former Quartermaster General of the Provisional IRA, to protest. More significantly perhaps was the other target of the crowd's ire — his long-term partner Bernadette Sands McKevitt. Her home in the nearby seaside suburb of Blackrock was picketed while she was driven out of her small business inside a Dundalk shopping centre. In the late summer of 1998 the unthinkable appeared to be happening. In Ireland, even in the deep green nationalist borderland of north Louth, a long-time haven for republicans who had fled Northern Ireland, the sister of Bobby Sands was a national hate figure seventeen years after her brother became the first hunger striker/martyr to die in the Maze death fast.

With the march on the McKevitts' home and the subsequent arrest of the Real IRA's founder, it appeared as if an organic movement was crystallising across the island that would force the final, complete end of the culture of 'armed struggle' in Ireland. In tandem with the groundswell of public anger post-Omagh, the dissident group sustained a series of stunning blows from the Irish security forces. In the first few years after the atrocity the Garda Síochána scored some notable successes in particular against the organisation. A measure of this was that ten years after the first Provisional IRA ceasefire there were around sixty inmates in Portlaoise top security prison allied to either the Real or Continuity IRAS; at the time of the 1994 cessation there were around forty Provo prisoners in the same jail. All the signs by the middle of the first decade of the twenty-first century were that the death cult of armed republicanism was coming to a terminus.

Omagh's agony is compounded by the fact that at the time of writing no one is likely ever to be charged in connection to the atrocity. This is in large part down to massive police incompetence on both sides of the border. Warnings about an imminent attack in the summer of 1998 from both the Republic of Ireland and Northern Ireland were ignored. Agony also turned to anger when it emerged that the security forces in both states had highly placed informants within the Real IRA which some of the victims' families allege were protected assets. Those that lost loved ones or were maimed for life in the bomb blast have every right to demand an independent public inquiry into the events before and after the massacre. However, by the beginning of 2008, now almost a decade later, their cause had been taken up by some of the Real IRA bombers' ex-comrades. When the Northern Ireland

Policing Board held two hours of discussion with PSNI Chief Constable Hugh Orde on 3 January 2008, Sinn Féin made sure their own moral indignation about the way the police in the North had mishandled the Omagh inquiry was amplified throughout a generally supine and unquestioning media.

Inside the claustrophobic rooms of the Policing Board's headquarters down at Belfast's Clarendon Dock, Sinn Féin's representatives, including Alex Maskey and Martina Anderson (herself a former bomber), were among those demanding truth and transparency from the PSNI over the bungled Omagh inquiry. On one level, of course, their presence there represented tangible political progress. Here were men and women who had tried to physically destroy the state now participating in one of that same state's most important new institutions. They were there too due to their electoral mandate, part of which was to hold the PSNI to account. Nevertheless it was still truly one of those surreal moments of the latter phase of the peace process — the political wing of the movement that had invented the car bomb and brought us Bloody Friday, the Abercorn, La Mon and Enniskillen was now demanding justice for the victims of the last major car bomb atrocity of the Troubles.

Despite Omagh, the 'deed' has been remarkably resilient even in the absence of any popular electoral mandate. Because just as the Edentubber dead drew their supposed legitimacy not from the ballot box but from the graves of those who had died before them in previous 'struggles', so the Real IRA and the Continuity IRA have argued with some plausibility that they could too. And from the vantage point of more than a dozen years after the first Provisional IRA ceasefire, the dissenters could also argue that the frenetic expectations raised back then by Gerry Adams et al have certainly not been fulfilled.

It certainly all seemed radically different on 31 August 1994, when there was a giant, open-air party thrown in west Belfast. A carnival had erupted all the way from the middle of the Andersonstown Road all the way down to the Lower Falls. There were cavalcades of black taxis tooting their horns. Tricolours were waved out of the shiny, dark, ubiquitous vehicles as well as from private cars. In addition to a forest of green, white and gold there were 'Good Luck' balloons, flowers, even teddy bears all clustered around Connolly House — the headquarters of Sinn Féin in Gerry Adams's heartland.

The festive atmosphere appeared infectious as hundreds upon hundreds of republicans took to the streets. Grown men hung out of moving motor cars screaming 'It's victory all right, it's victory', while others stopped reporters covering the scenes to shout: 'Don't go to work. Today's a holiday. They'll be calling it St Gerry's Day in a few years' time.'

Rides in the black cabs were free and pints in pubs and clubs controlled by the Provisionals cost just 25p, presumably the 1969 price of a beer. Even beyond west Belfast it seemed people, including journalists, were getting caught up in the euphoria. Inside BBC Northern Ireland's newsroom in Belfast's Ormeau Avenue, for instance, one senior correspondent even suggested that now was the time for everyone who didn't have one to apply for an Irish passport as a United Ireland wasn't far off.

The day the Provisional IRA ended their armed campaign (or so it seemed) was taken to mark a victory for republicans. Even British newspaper leader writers were losing the run of their reason. *The Guardian*, for instance, suggested 'the logic of disengagement is in motion, fuelling loyalist fears. For Britain too there can be no going back.'

Some unionists were already falling into that same trap. James, later Lord, Molyneaux had already described the peace process as one of the most dangerous periods for the Union in its history. Across unionist areas of Ulster there was a sneaking suspicion that the Provos hadn't just relinquished the armed struggle for nothing; that there had to be a secret deal that would end in the Union being broken. Yet ironically it was those whom the likes of Molyneaux regarded as the lowest in the unionist food-chain, the loyalist paramilitaries, who had a clearer and more accurate picture of what actually was going on that day.

Within twelve hours of the IRA cessation the Ulster Volunteer Force sent out its street-painters to issue a message of reassurance to working-class loyalists. On strategic locations along the Shankill Road and east Belfast they left a series of thank you notes to the IRA:

'On behalf of the loyalist people the Ulster Volunteer Force would like to accept the unconditional surrender of the IRA,' one read on a wall close to The Eagle, the UVF's head-quarters on the middle of the Shankill Road.

It wasn't exactly a surrender at all yet, nor had the IRA ended their campaign with any real sense of tangible victory. Behind the smiles, republican strategists such as Danny Morrison offered a more sober if somewhat contradictory analysis of where the IRA now was. Morrison told *The Guardian's* David Sharrock: 'Armed struggle has not failed, but it has not worked either.' This curious A and -A logic certainly reflected the confused state of republicans as they entered this new, uncharted era.

In the same edition of *The Guardian*, the paper's South African correspondent David Beresford wrote an intelligent piece comparing and contrasting the fortunes of the IRA with the ANC. On page 4 Beresford noted: 'The parallels between South Africa and Northern Ireland are, however, shaky.' While Beresford warned the readers of the daily liberal British bible about the spurious comparisons between the transition from Apartheid and the Irish peace process, the *Guardian* appeared to think that the IRA would never go back to war.

'In the end it is hard to dispute Albert Reynolds' conclusion in the Dáil yesterday, that for the IRA there can now be no going back.'

Everyone, it seemed, in the British and Irish media got carried away with the idea that somehow the IRA had secured a secret deal from the British government that would lead to disengagement from Northern Ireland.

The *Guardian* appeared to believe that the loyalists would not call off their violence, predicting that they would continue to kill even though a ceasefire was more or less inevitable from the UVF and UDA despite a summer of Provo provocations and ongoing UVF and UDA sectarian assassinations.

From the first day of the ceasefire through to the loyalist cessation in October and beyond into Christmas, Northern Ireland enjoyed a honeymoon era of peace. But the political expectations of mainstream republicanism and unionism remained as far apart as ever, and in the case of the former, wildly over-optimistic. This was clearly on display at Sinn Féin's first Ard Fheis held in Dublin on 25 February 1995.

The two keynote addresses as ever were from the party's

Chief Negotiator Martin McGuinness and party President Gerry Adams. First up came McGuinness and he had an uncompromising message for the faithful.

'There can no going back,' he announced to a confident arena. 'Partition has failed and there can be no return to a Stormont regime. Sinn Féin's attitude to Stormont is one of abstention. There can be no involvement by republicans in any body which denies the right of the people of this island to national self-determination.' Just three years later the policy of abstentionism at Stormont would go the same way as that of the Dáil in 1986, that is, it would be ditched unceremoniously, with hardly a protest from the rank and file.

There were, however, faint hints in McGuiness's speech that the emerging New Sinn Féin might be more flexible: 'Republicans will, of course, consider transitional arrangements which are linked to a clear commitment by the British government to end British jurisdiction in our country.' McGuinness ended his address to the conference with an intangible promise of change ahead.

'The old order must fall — a new day must dawn. Until then the ship will remain steady in the water — the tide of history is flowing with us to our journey's end.'

It all sounded as dreamy and ethereal as a lyric from an Enya album, although couched behind the poetical prophecy was an appeal for faith and unity from the republican base.

The following day the other side in this remarkable political double act took to the podium in Dublin's Mansion House, from where in the late 1980s Sinn Féin had once been banned.

Gerry Adams devoted two pages of a sixteen-page speech

to the IRA. He harked back to the day of the ceasefire and noted that the families of two old Ballymurphy comrades, Jim Bryson and Pat Mulvenna, had been among the crowds of well-wishers outside Connolly House. Adams then maintained the party line that the IRA had not lost the war.

'To sue for peace is a noble thing . . . undertaken by a confident, united and unbroken army.'

In a speech peppered with the new vocabulary of post-1994 Sinn Féin — 'parity of esteem', 'equality of treatment' etc — Adams still spoke over the heads of unionists towards the British government. He again urged the British to become 'persuaders of Irish unity', a phrase this writer first heard mentioned by a key republican supporter in the Dublin print media four years earlier.

Adams also took heart in the publication that month of the British and Irish governments' 'Frameworks Document', an outline of the political way forward that suggested North-South bodies that would assume quasi-governmental functions. These bodies would not come under the final control of an Assembly based in Belfast. Indeed the Irish Republic's then Foreign Minister David Andrews raised unionist fears by claiming these bodies would 'not be unlike a government'. The London *Times* seemed to agree with this analysis, claiming that the document 'brings the prospect of a United Ireland closer than it had been at any time since partition'. The President of Sinn Féin concurred with this view, which gave his base great encouragement.

'The Framework[s] Document is a discussion document. But its publication by the two governments is a clear recognition that partition has failed.'

Both the unionists and the IRA and Sinn Féin membership

drew the same conclusion — 'Frameworks' had been the price the governments were prepared to pay for the Provisionals' cessation of violence just six months earlier. Its publication cost Jim Molyneaux his job as the leader of the Ulster Unionists (he was charged with putting too much faith in John Major) and it led to the first major split in loyalism, the defection of the majority of the UVF's Mid Ulster Brigade led by Billy 'King Rat' Wright. It also produced hard-line unionist graffiti in the UVF's east Belfast. Under the slogan 'The Union is Safe', the loyalist dissidents wrote with bitter irony 'Ha Ha Ha.'

Three years later, however, the Ulster Unionists led by David Trimble in negotiations with Irish nationalism actually managed to severely dilute the cross-border elements of 'Frameworks'. One of the 1995 document's authors had been the former head of the Northern Ireland Civil Service, Sir David Fell. In a forensic comparative study of 'Frameworks' versus 'The Belfast Agreement', Sir David noted that cross-border bodies had been 'executive' under 'Frameworks' whereas in the Good Friday Agreement these institutions via the North/South Ministerial Council were now there 'to develop consultation, co-operation and action within the island of Ireland . . .' The North-South overarching body would not have any clear distinct identity under the Belfast Agreement. Nor could its powers evolve and strengthen. Instead these bodies would be answerable to the Northern Ireland Assembly and the Dáil, and each would have a veto over them. The actual number of bodies was also dramatically slashed to just six from more than a dozen in the 1995 document. Moreover, key Sinn Féin demands back in 1995 such as policing and courts coming under a cross-border justice agency were not realised. Sir David, who had been a key architect of 'Frameworks', concluded that the Agreement posed far less of a threat to unionism than the 1995 blueprint he had helped draw up. And in addition, Articles 2 and 3 of the Irish Republic's Constitution — the national legal imperative to take back the Fourth Green Field — had been scrapped by an overwhelming vote in the Southern Irish part of the referendum to endorse the Good Friday Agreement. Indeed even before the Agreement was signed in early 1998 Sinn Féin's new, principal ally, the publisher Niall O'Dowd, spotted the dangers for republicans contained in this outline of the Good Friday deal, the 'Heads of Agreement' published by the British and Irish governments as a kind of precursor of the actual agreement. In O'Dowd's opinion, this pre-outline of what was to become the Good Friday Accord gave Sinn Féin 'very little satisfaction'. The two governments, O'Dowd complained, had moved away from the 'Frameworks' document. He was absolutely correct in his assessment.

Back in 1995 republicans were still engaging in the politics of illusion. For instance, other senior delegates to the first post-ceasefire Ard Fheis had even more ambitious blueprints than 'Frameworks' which they contended could edge the North into a United Ireland. Veteran Adams ally Tom Hartley put forward a discussion paper at the conference which explored the concept of 'transitional arrangements'. This included what the West Belfast city councillor described as a 'transitional charter' mapping the way forward.

'This charter will be implemented within a period of not more than ten years (the transitional period),' Hartley told his fellow comrades.

There would also be, he suggested, a Review Conference for political arrangements on the island. This would be carried out under the auspices of bodies like the Council of Europe, the Committee for Security and Co-operation in Europe and even the UN. Hartley envisaged that this process would lay 'the possible foundations for the process of national reconciliation', which he even hinted in his paper might be administered jointly by the CSCE and the Americans.

There are several interesting elements to Hartley's concept that need to be unpicked in our search for reasons why the 'deed' refuses to go away. The first is the time-frame, 'not more than ten years', already a retreat from the maximalist goal of short-term British disengagement. Hartley, one of those who has, to his credit, been stalking the lost deed for longer than most inside the Provisionals, also seemed prepared to swap one set of alien rulers (the hated Brits) with several others, namely the European bureaucracy and the Clinton Administration, albeit for a limited period of time.

The Sinn Féin leadership had been wooing Clinton ever since the Democrats returned to power in 1992. Indeed republican strategists, most crucially Adams himself, had urged Irish America to entice the Clinton White House into a political pincer movement comprised of the USA, Britain and Ireland, that would exert enough pressure on the unionists to accept some sort of transitional arrangement leading to Irish unity, not so much by consent but rather by external unarmed co-coercion.

In order to enlist American co-operation into this project, Adams and co. had to severely dilute their previous rhetoric regarding the world's only remaining superpower. Only four years before Clinton came to power, Adams's own attitude towards the USA was markedly different from the one he adopted during the coming 'Billary' era.

In *A Pathway to Peace* published by the Mercier Press in 1988, Adams engaged in traditional anti-American imperialist rhetoric on the sleeve of his book.

'Britain does not act alone — the British claim to the territory of Ireland is stressed by the American and Western European concern to maintain the status quo especially because of the strategic location of Ireland.'

Just one year before the collapse of communism and the end of the Cold War, Adams was waving his clenched fist not only at British colonialism but also towards those neo-colonialists in the US as he portrayed Ireland as if it was some kind of potential rain-drenched Cuba that could threaten NATO's western flank.

All this old leftist anti-American rhetoric was eventually junked as part of the strategy of building a tri-partite governmental front that would advance Sinn Féin's goals. This would lead the party eventually into unknown and unwelcome territory. By the time Clinton had vacated the White House and been replaced by George W. Bush, the Adams project was so reliant on American pressure being applied on their British allies that Sinn Féin leaders were shaking hands with the US Republican President inside the splendour of Hillsborough Castle while Irish leftists and peace activists protested outside against the invasion of Iraq and the overthrow of the Ba'athist dictatorship in early 2003.

Dumping the anti-American, anti-imperialist chic was part of a plan to use the Americans to politically encircle unionism. But at the end of more than a decade of political negotiations, culminating in the St Andrews Agreement of 2006, the decision to wrap themselves up with the Stars and Stripes ended up instead becoming a trap for the republican movement.

The Clinton administration had stood accused of at best being biased in favour of the Sinn Féin-driven nationalist agenda and at worst of turning a blind eye to ongoing acts of IRA violence and criminality. The best example of the latter was the 1999 Florida gunrunning plot in which several IRA members were arrested in the Sunshine State for illegally buying handguns that they were shipping back to Northern Ireland. FBI agents and RUC investigators working with them in Florida later revealed that they came under enormous pressure from senior figures in the Clinton White House to publicly deny any IRA link to the smuggling operation, which supplied the Provisionals with more than 100 new, forensically clean handguns. (These 'clean' weapons would allow the Provos to continue to murder opponents and petty criminals but would have no forensic history and thus no trace back to the IRA.)

Once in the White House, however, President Bush and his team adopted a much more sceptical, wary approach to the republican movement and they certainly had good grounds for their caution.

In the months before the 9/11 attacks on New York and Washington DC, the Americans were dealing with another terrorist problem in South America — the FARC armed campaign in Colombia. The hard-line Marxist insurgency group funded its fight to overthrow the elected government in Bogotá by becoming a major player in the cocaine trade. So not only did FARC threaten the stability of a key South

American ally, the guerilla group was in part responsible for the flood of the drug into North America. When three Irish republicans, all long-standing allies of the Sinn Féin leadership, turned up in Colombia, where they had been FARC's guests, the Americans went apoplectic with rage. This rage reached its climax on the very day Al Qaeda attacked America, with Bush's then envoy to Northern Ireland, Richard Haas, leading from the front.

Haas had flown into Dublin to meet a number of key players in the peace process, most notably Martin McGuinness and Gerry Adams. It was during an encounter with the Sinn Féin chief negotiators that Haas lost his patience. Armed with intelligence reports from the CIA, Haas knew exactly what the IRA had been up to. After a few minutes listening to Adams talking about 'inching forward' the political process, Haas finally snapped.

'If any American, service personnel or civilian, is killed in Colombia by the technology the IRA supplied then you can fuck off,' he shouted, finger jabbing towards Adams's chest. 'Don't tell me you know nothing about what's going on there, we know everything about it.'

Haas, eyes blazing, was referring to events a month earlier when the three Irishmen, including two IRA veterans, were arrested at Bogotá airport. They were returning from a trip to FARCland, a Marxist ruritania in Colombia.

James Monaghan and Martin McAuley, two IRA engineers, were swapping mortar bomb technology with the FARC guerrillas. FARC was and is the sworn enemy of America and controls the land used to cultivate and export cocaine to the West. Haas was furious.

Paradoxically the discovery of the trip was the lever

America needed to push Adams towards the historic announcement that the IRA had agreed to decommission some of its weapons, a move that was sealed by David Trimble's decision to return to government as Northern Ireland's First Minister.

A few hours later on 9/11 when the first of four hijacked planes flew into the World Trade Centre, Sinn Féin must have known they were on an impossible wicket.

The process had actually started back in July 2001. Around a large oval table at the Weston Park country house hotel in Shropshire, Jonathan Powell, Tony Blair's Chief of Staff, told Adams they were reaching the 'take it or leave it stage' of the peace process. Blair had ordered the leaders of Sinn Féin, the Ulster Unionists and the SDLP to the closed talks to tell them that the peace process was in danger of withering on the vine. Powell told Adams that the IRA needed to move, and move fast.

But at that stage Sinn Féin was in no hurry. Adams probably knew that decommissioning had to come but was struggling with hard-line members of the IRA. Brian Keenan, a leading member of the IRA's ruling council, had said it was the British state that should be decommissioning its military presence, not them.

Such was the lack of political progress that both Adams and Trimble took time off from the 'crisis summit' to go to London — Adams for a speech, Trimble to go to a garden party. Downing Street muttered darkly that the approach of some of the protagonists was bordering on the cavalier.

The FARC debacle and 11 September 2001 completely changed the landscape. Adams's principal concern remained the maintenance of warm relations with the American administration and the preservation of the supply of millions of dollars from rich, conservative Irish-Americans.

The Sinn Féin leader was in little doubt about the mood change in America. Bill Flynn, a close confidant of Irish nationalists and republicans, was one of the pivotal figures in Irish-American politics and, as chairman of the Mutual Bank of America, was a conservative that no government in Washington could afford to ignore. Flynn made it clear to Adams and Sinn Féin after Colombia that the only way to rescue the party's reputation in the US capital was for the IRA to disarm. 'They listen to me because they know I am a strong supporter of what they are doing to unite Ireland,' he later told *The Observer* newspaper in late September 2001.

Flynn was the figurehead for a group of American businessmen sympathetic to Sinn Féin, who were simultaneously crucial to fund-raising while also pushing for an end to the military campaign. In 2000 alone the party raised more than $1 million from corporate Irish-American backers and Adams had realised that, such was the gravity of the situation, Sinn Féin risked having to close its crucial Washington office.

'It wasn't just me,' Flynn said, admitting that he would need to 'pull out a calendar' to remember the large number of times he had communicated with Adams over the past few weeks. 'It was a number of executives who saw those relationships with the Colombians as devastating. Colombia is a place that peddles drugs into this country.'

Flynn spoke to Adams through a series of communiqués couriered by personal envoys, both men too nervous of being bugged to use the telephone. Flynn was clear. 'They [in Washington] are not going to put up with any more nonsense,' he said. 'After Colombia and then September 11 the time had come for real politics, and we had got to decommission.'

Which is exactly what occurred on 26 September 2005 with the first major act of disarmament in front of the eyes of General de Chastelain and his officials. American pressure proved paramount.

The disjunction between how the Bush White House saw the developing political process and the way the British and Irish governments went out of their way to placate Sinn Féin became even more pronounced after Richard Haas's departure as the President's Special Envoy to Northern Ireland. Haas's successor, Mitchell Reiss, was even less inclined to take Sinn Féin's word or promote their cause to the detriment of the unionists. Evidence of this is contained in a virtually unreported academic study of the Bush Administration's Northern Ireland policy between 2001 and 2006.

US academic Mary Alice Clancy spoke to senior members of the Bush White House intimately involved in the negotiations that finally led to the St Andrews deal. She made several interesting observations about the White House officials regarding Northern Ireland. The first was what they wanted to get out of the Irish process. Clancy concluded that the Bush Presidency was more interested in British counter-intelligence and anti-insurgent techniques against the IRA than the use of political compromise. They were particularly keen to draw lessons in their battle to stabilise post-Saddam Iraq.

This was the first major academic survey into the Bush effect on Northern Ireland politics and the pressure thus applied on the Provisionals. Clancy interviewed nine US State Department officials and she noted that: 'They were interested in how the British not only infiltrated the IRA but also shaped policy; how they promoted and encouraged those emerging in the movement that were more realistic, the ones who realised they could not win the war. I think that is the central lesson they, the US State Department officials I talked to, believed they could draw for Iraq,' she later recalled.

She argued, with quite a degree of justification, that the Bush Administration in fact played a central role in the St Andrews Agreement, which led to the restoration of devolution in May 2007. The deal that led to a once unthinkable coalition headed up by Ian Paisley and Martin McGuinness rested on a cornerstone — Sinn Féin signing up to support the police and the judicial system within Northern Ireland. And, according to Clancy, that cornerstone was the work of Reiss and others in the Bush White House.

Sinn Féin's willingness to support the Police Service of Northern Ireland was the key test for Paisley and his party that mainstream republicans had given up violence for good. Clancy said that those she spoke to in the State Department insisted it was Reiss who pursued this pre-condition to power-sharing far more vigorously than either the British or Irish governments. Reiss resisted overturning George Bush's ban on Sinn Féin raising funds in the United States the previous summer in the build-up to the St Andrew's talks. Dermot Ahern, the Irish Foreign Minister, had tried to persuade the Americans to soften their stance on policing as the price for power-sharing. The US Special Envoy maintained that the ban would only be lifted once Sinn Féin agreed to sign up to policing.

One US official told Clancy the reported rift during the summer of 2006 between Reiss and the then Northern

Ireland Secretary Peter Hain over the policing pre-condition was also real.

'I think they [the British government] went after Mitchell harder than they went after Richard Haas [Bush's previous Envoy]. Because when Mitchell started to actually continue to insist that policing mattered and we restricted Gerry Adams' visa for fund-raising, it was much tougher with British officials, and open and nasty. . . . They were much more angry at Mitchell last year. I mean that was really icky,' the State Department source said.

Reiss insisted to both the British and Irish governments that Paisley would not sign up to the deal at St Andrew's without a Sinn Féin commitment to support the police and the rule of law in Northern Ireland. So eventually, at the start of 2007, in a sequenced prelude to devolution being restored to Stormont, Sinn Féin held a special conference and unanimously endorsed support for the PSNI. (Once again the vote underlined the power Adams really exercised over the base, despite constant protestations from himself and others in the leadership that they had to take their time for fear of rupture.)

Although the DUP only backed the St Andrew's deal after the policing pre-condition was met, the State Department and British officials interviewed by Clancy revealed that Paisley was already prepared to share power with Sinn Féin before the accord.

The Bush and Blair governments were also at odds over the latter's view of 'ordinary' IRA crime such as robberies. One American official told Clancy:

'This was the biggest irritant between us and the Northern Ireland Office. I don't believe that they [the NIO] had ever

issued a policy statement to the police to tell them to ignore
IRA criminality as long as it did not turn into bombs on the
mainland, but I believe that many, many police thought they
operated under those rules.'

The alleged British policy of 'turning a blind eye' in the
interests of the wider peace process, the American official
added, ended after the IRA stole £26 million in the Northern
Bank raid. Following the robbery the Americans adopted a
told-you-so attitude to their NIO counterparts, he said.

'What did you just train the IRA to do? You [the NIO] told
them that they can carry out egregious, blatant criminal
behaviour in the run up to an election, and we will turn a
blind eye to it. So then you know what? They came back and
did the Northern Bank,' the State Department said, summing
up what he and his colleagues had said to the NIO.

Even after St Andrews the British government continued
to try and water down the policing element to the deal in
order not to cause the Sinn Féin leadership any grief from its
base. Almost exactly one year after that historic agreement,
Ian Paisley returned to Scotland, this time to the west coast.
In his capacity as First Minister of Northern Ireland Paisley
was guest of honour at the opening of the Wigtown
International Book Festival held every year in the first
weekend of September.

After opening the conference, Paisley revealed to me, in
the back stage of a marquee tent shortly after the DUP leader's
address to the books festival, that Tony Blair was still trying
to dilute the policing requirement so insisted upon by the
Americans. The DUP leader said that on New Year's Day 2007
he was woken up in bed by a phone call from the then Prime
Minister who was on a post-Christmas holiday in the

Caribbean. There was only one item on the agenda, Paisley
said: Blair implored him to allow modifications to the
policing section of the St Andrew's Agreement. Paisley
refused and tried to get back to sleep. To no avail. Blair made
a further five phone calls that morning attempting to
persuade Paisley to backtrack a little on the policing
question. Each time Paisley refused to relent.

The timing of these New Year's Day calls was critical —
within less than a month Sinn Féin was to hold a special Ard
Fheis/conference which would either ratify or reject support
for the Police Service of Northern Ireland. Blair, according to
Paisley's version of events, was again trying to cut Sinn Féin
some slack. The problem, however, was that just like the
republican movement's relationship to the United States, the
dynamics of British and Northern Irish politics had also
altered radically. Paisley was unmoved by prime ministerial
pressure. He would and could not relent on policing and
Sinn Féin's support for the PSNI as the republicans' passport
into power-sharing. Otherwise Paisley knew he would split
the DUP down the middle.

Moreover Blair no longer exercised such a mesmeric
charm on the unionist political leadership. He was a lame
duck Prime Minister whom everyone, including Paisley,
knew was about to hand over the reins of power to Gordon
Brown. The result of the Ard Fheis vote, an overwhelming
vote in favour, also exposed the charade the Adams
leadership had dazzled Blair and his Downing Street Chief of
Staff Jonathan Powell with for so long. The true balance of
forces, contrary to the opinions of Blair and Powell, within
the Provisionals was always heavily loaded in Adams's favour.
Despite the departure of a handful of former prominent

activists such as Jim McAllister and Davy Hyland from South Armagh, the vast majority of Sinn Féin was still under Adams's tight control. Perhaps Paisley too guessed that Adams would easily win the day. He no longer cared about Blair's concern for Adams's leadership and its survival. Moreover, the DUP leader now had America on his side in the policing debate.

What all this indicates is that the Sinn Féin strategy of uniting Dublin, London and Washington DC against unionism was spent. Of course, once Sinn Féin signed up to the new policing structures the doors to the White House were open again.

In parallel to wooing Capitol Hill, Sinn Féin's leadership had already ditched decades of anti-imperalist, radical chic sloganising and embraced the largesse of US capitalism. The party had sought to boost its war chest with millions of dollars in donations from corporate America. The trouble was that once the party and the IRA appeared to be regressing into its old leftist anti-colonialist mode (as witnessed in Colombia with FARC and in Cuba with the constant sucking up to the Castro dictatorship) their new financial backers recoiled in horror. The hard-headed realists in New Sinn Féin had a choice: either retreat back into leftist certainties to appease their radical fringe or do what their new financial supporters in North America wanted them to do, namely decommission. With the stick of White House sanctions post 9/11 and the blunder-in-the-Colombian-jungle hanging over them, as well as the carrot of US corporate finance dangling in front of them, the leadership chose the latter option. As always with the Provisionals' leadership, most significantly of all with

Adams, Sinn Féin's leftist hangers-on were entirely expendable. They could sell heaps of Che Guevara T-shirts from their stalls at universities and take self-indulgent nostalgia trips to Cuba for their holidays, but in the end they would be unceremoniously dumped along with their policies in the interests of realpolitik, Provo-style.

To those the Adams/McGuinness leadership had long left behind, especially Ruairí Ó Brádaigh and his loyal band of die-hards in Republican Sinn Féin, it must have all resembled that infamous scene at the end of *Animal Farm* when the beasts who have been excluded from the pigs' rapprochement with the men look on and are unable to distinguish between porcine and human. While Friends of Sinn Féin hosted $1,000 per plate fund-raising dinners in Manhattan five-star hotels, Ó Brádaigh could only address the handful of ballot sellers and street collectors for RSF in America via a webcam address from Ireland; the president of that party had been banned from the United States. There was even worse in store for the Real IRA, which after 9/11 was put on a par with terrorist organisations like Al Qaeda, Hamas and Hezbollah. The Real IRA and its support group, the 32-County Sovereignty Committee, were designated as banned organisations in the US. Even Bernadette Sands McKevitt was reduced to the status of Islamist firebrands like Mohammed Omar Bakri and also banned from the United States. The dissidents of all hues had found themselves on the wrong side of the fence when it came to Bush-the-younger's 'war on terror'. In contrast, Adams was far more astute and pragmatic in realising that global politics had shifted on its axis after the 9/11 attacks.

Just four years before the 1994 ceasefire, veterans and

current activists from the Provos' 1st Battalion of the Belfast Brigade in the west of the city decided to commemorate their exploits over the previous two decades. They brought out a booklet called *20 Years of Struggle* and in the preface of that publication an unnamed author made this telling prediction.

'If we were to fail or falter in this final phase of National Liberation then we shall, in the immortal words of our own the late Máire Drumm, be haunted by the ghosts of our patriot dead. To their comrades we simply say "fight on, we are with you".'

For most of the twentieth century the dead exercised as much, arguably even more, influence as the living over Irish politics. From Patrick Pearse's graveside oration about the British fools leaving 'us our patriot dead' at O'Donovan Rossa's funeral to the beatification of the 1981 hunger strikers, the debt owed to the dead generations has been like a form of malign social gravity, pulling everything down into the mire of history. Back in 1969/70 the Provisionals revived a death cult that appeared to be flickering out, no longer casting such a predominant shadow as Ireland rapidly modernised in the late Sixties. Yet that cult's re-emergence back at the end of that most optimistic decade demonstrated that it is a social force with an enduring if at times dwindling band of followers.

So those now stalking the 'deed' are unable to finally exorcise the ghosts they conjured up from the grave when they deployed such ressurectionist metaphors as the PIRA Phoenix rising from the ashes of 1969. Today there are no more burned-down Bombay Streets out of whose embers a new Phoenix can arise. But there are none the less ghosts still swirling around, called back out of their resting places to howl again at the living and to implore the deed to stalk those seeking to bring it to a final conclusion. Judging by the outcome of twelve years of negotiations following the 1994 ceasefires, the 'final phase of National Liberation' mentioned in the 1st Battalion's pamphlet has undoubtedly failed. The warning from the late Máire Drumm, the one-time Madame Mao of the Provisional IRA, remains a potent and dangerous one.

Another PIRA founder and veteran who lived to see 'the final phase of National Liberation' fizzle out was John 'Blue' Kelly. One of the defendants in the 1970 Arms Trial, Kelly became one of the most amiable characters to emerge from within the Provisionals. At the end of his political career Kelly would also become one of the most honest, although his candour would eventually result in him too being cast into the political wilderness by the leadership.

In the autumn of 2005, as he was being treated for prostate cancer, the South Derry republican reflected back on the split in which he had played such a central part back in 1969 and in particular the nascent Provos' coup d'etat against the Goulding loyalists in Belfast.

In an interview in September 2005 in *The Blanket* e-zine run by ex-IRA prisoner Anthony McIntyre, Kelly reached this startlingly honest conclusion. Thinking about that schism at the genesis of the Troubles, he admitted: 'The leadership [i.e. Billy McMillen] in Belfast were reluctant to engage because of their own political philosophy; maybe they were right at the end of the day. Maybe at the end of the day things would have gone better if they had prevailed, but at the time it was just how you could procure the weaponry.'

There is surely no more damning indictment of the futility of the 'armed struggle' than this, coming from the lips of one of the Provisionals' alpha-men. They wanted guns first and foremost; thinking through the implications of launching their bloody adventure was for wimps.

Epilogue
2016 Postponed

Throughout the second half of the 1990s right up until early into the twenty-first century, at every Irish election, both local and national, the main hall of Dublin's main RDS conference centre echoed to the triumphalist cheering and chanting of the republican movement. Legions of Sinn Féin activists, mainly young men, marked the election of party candidates with wild clapping, the waving of the Irish Tricolour and the singing of songs celebrating the exploits of the Provisional IRA.

But on Friday 25 May 2007 there was virtual silence from the Sinn Féin faithful inside the place where the party leadership had recently staged so many carefully choreographed post-ceasefire conferences. On that weekend the knots of Sinn Féin activists were almost entirely subdued. Some were visibly shocked over what they were hearing and seeing. Sinn Féin TDs such as Sean Crowe were losing their seats while targeted constituencies were failing to return hotly tipped candidates including Pearse Doherty. Even

Gerry Adams appeared unable to explain what was happening.

The party's reversal in fortunes was most personified by the fate of Mary Lou McDonald, who had stood in Bertie Ahern's home constituency, Dublin Central. For nearly a decade McDonald had become a near permanent feature beside Gerry Adams on his visits to Government Buildings in Dublin, the Stormont estate in Belfast, Number 10 Downing Street and the White House. This telegenic, good-looking, articulate Trinity College Dublin graduate (a former member of Fianna Fáil while a student at the university) was, alongside Pearse Doherty, the epitome of the new Sinn Féin. An MEP for Dublin, McDonald was also tasked with perhaps the most important strategic target of the election to the 30th Dáil — to knock out the Taoiseach's running mate in Dublin and snatch a seat off Fianna Fáil.

As the count came early on Friday morning McDonald started to look crestfallen. When all the votes were in, she had polled just 3,182 first preference votes, a tally far short of being in contention for the last seat of the north inner city constituency.

The supreme irony of her electoral performance was that McDonald had been parachuted into the constituency to replace the previous candidate, Sinn Féin's Nicky Kehoe. The former IRA man had come tantalisingly close to taking a seat off Fianna Fáil in the 2002 election. Kehoe, the embodiment of old Sinn Féin with his IRA past, including prison sentences for kidnap, came within 76 votes of entering the Dáil at Fianna Fáil's expense. By the end of 2007 Kehoe had resigned from the party, an indication that he and others around him in the area had become disillusioned and embittered by their leadership's decision to ditch one of the movement's most loyal cadres for this relative newcomer.

What made the overall Sinn Féin reverse all the more stunning was that during the election campaign the party was enjoying favourable publicity across Ireland and beyond. The poll came just three weeks after Sinn Féin entered a power-sharing government with Ian Paisley in Belfast. The Republic of Ireland was, according to the script, meant to display its gratitude to McGuinness, Adams et al and reward the party with a place in another government. Instead the Irish electorate's ingratitude underlined a fundamental fact about politics on the island — there were two states which were and still are very much places apart.

The historic setback in the Republic failed to wipe the smile off the face of Martin McGuinness, however, who throughout the second half of 2007 appeared to be really enjoying the job as Northern Ireland's Deputy First Minister. The epithet of 'Chuckle Brothers' bestowed on McGuinness and Paisley as they beamed and smiled all the way from Wall Street to a new Ikea store near Belfast City Airport symbolised the pragmatic, working relationship at Stormont between the former bitter adversaries. The double-act also transmitted a message that the power-sharing arrangement dominated by the DUP and Sinn Féin remained solid at least for the time being.

However, events or as the Israelis call them, 'facts on the ground', have a nasty habit of changing the political atmosphere in Northern Ireland. One particular event in the autumn of 2007 in South Armagh was to prove that the unlikely coalition between old Provos and Paisleyites could still be shaken to its foundations.

Paul Quinn was born into a South Armagh that was effectively at war. In 1986, the year of his birth, there was no visible indication that the 'armed struggle' was coming to a close, that the IRA was prepared to put away the gun and bomb, or that the British army was prepared to scale down its pervasive presence across the region from hilltop fortresses to Europe's busiest military heli-pad. However, by the time he reached twenty-one the Cullyhanna man was living in an age of supposed peace, where even the party that had displaced the SDLP as the hegemonic force in the constituency, Sinn Féin, was now supporting the police.

Quinn had been involved in a series of brawls with young men who came from well-connected republican families in Cullyhanna as well as nearby Cullaville and Crossmaglen. He had got the better of two men both related to former IRA prisoners and for this he faced the ignominious prospect of having to leave his native South Armagh and go into exile. The expulsion order in the summer of 2007 had been imposed by local commanders of the Provisional IRA. Naively perhaps Quinn had believed that with the mainstream republican movement embracing policing he could afford to snub the exile order. He decided to stay in defiance of the local IRA and for this he would pay with his life.

On Saturday afternoon, 20 October 2007, Paul Quinn received a mobile phone call from some friends. They summoned him to a cow shed just across the border in County Monaghan, but what Quinn did not know was that their call was a trap. His two friends had been taken hostage in a carefully planned, well-executed kidnap operation involving at least a dozen men using a series of vans. So when

Paul Quinn arrived he was set upon by at least ten of the gang and dragged inside to the shed. The friends who had been used to lure him to the remote farm building listened in horror as they heard the screams and cries of Paul Quinn being beaten savagely. They later reported to Quinn's family that during the prolonged assault his attackers kept shouting out loud, no doubt for their benefit, that 'we are the bosses around here'. It was a message the beating was meant to transmit: no one, regardless of ceasefires or Agreements or power-sharing Executives, would challenge the authority of the IRA's South Armagh brigade. The 'lesson' delivered by the gang ended with Paul Quinn's death, probably an unintentional result of a merciless beating. Indeed, his injuries were so severe that one Garda officer later on the scene reported that Quinn's body 'looked like a lump of jelly'. Among those delivering the so-called 'punishment beating' was someone extremely close to a senior and rising star of Sinn Féin. In fact, this man may have delivered the fatal blow after striking Paul Quinn on the head with a crowbar. Whether Quinn died from that one strike or from a multiplicity of injuries, the presence of this young man, a native of Cullaville, should have had profound political consequences.

Within days of the Quinn murder and the subsequent allegations from his family that the local Provisional IRA carried it out, Sinn Féin leaders, including the area's MP, Conor Murphy, sought to portray the killing as a product of a clash between rival criminals in South Armagh. This explanation was an uncanny re-run of Sinn Féin's attempt to explain away the events inside and outside Magennis's Bar on the night Robert McCartney died. Sinn Féin's then representative Joe O'Donnell claimed that the fatal stabbing had been yet another example of the new, deadly knife culture afflicting parts of Northern Ireland. And as with the McCartney murder, so it would transpire in the Quinn case such 'explanations' would turn out to be both spurious and threadbare.

At the time of writing, however, there is no prospect that the Quinn killing will itself bring down the power-sharing executive at Stormont. To put it most cynically, why would Ian Paisley, the new leader of unionism, sacrifice what is essentially a partitionist settlement because of one murder in republican South Armagh, affecting people who would never be likely to support him or his party? Political reality will dictate that the Paul Quinn murder won't alter the balance of forces at Stormont in the short to medium term.

A far greater tragedy than that particularly brutal South Armagh IRA brigade killing is the overall futility of what was once known as the 'armed struggle'. That campaign was also once described as 'armed propaganda', in essence a series of political acts of advertising, to remind the world that the conflict was unresolved, to warn their enemies of what they were capable of doing. But for the last three and a half decades the IRA's message was constantly being delivered to the wrong address. It took the Provisionals thirty-five years to acknowledge that those they should be talking to, the real 'British presence' in Ireland, were those that still call themselves British. The trouble is that this ideological turnaround may have come too late. After having spent decades trying to bomb the unionists into a United Ireland, the Provos' latest message to unionists of peace and fraternal love looks likely to be spurned. Like the Irish electorate in the

2007 general election, the Ulster Protestants too are going to
'return to sender'.

So what kind of conflict did Ireland endure in the years
between 1969 and 1997? Could it in any way be categorised as
a 'war'? At present a de facto Truth Commission headed by a
former Catholic priest and an ex-Anglican Primate of All
Ireland are engaged in the tortuous process of unpicking our
recent bloodsoaked past. Denis Bradley and Robin Eames
head up an independent body given the Herculean task of
exploring the truths and the distortions of the last thirty-five
plus years. In the first week of 2008 they caused immediate
controversy by suggesting that the time was probably right
for the British government to declare that they had been at
war with the Provisional IRA. The idea instantly produced the
usual bi-polarity in the political process. Unionists
denounced the concept as dangerous nonsense, which if
taken up would somehow legitimise what the PIRA had been
involved in, whereas republicans appeared to rejoice over the
notion that they would soon be re-defined in history as
soldiers who had just fought a 'war' and (even more
ludicrously) ended with a score-draw against the British.

As always in Northern Ireland, none of the representatives
of the two main political blocs had thought through the
unintended consequences of re-designating the Troubles as
'war'. For republicans there are particular dangers lurking
behind what on the surface must appear to them to be an
alluring concept. If, officially, the British state recognises that
it was a war, then this entails that all sides are potentially
vulnerable to the charge of war crimes. Thus Bloody Sunday
was a war crime, while the loyalist paramilitaries' deliberate
targeting of Catholic civilians was, under the articles of war,

also a series of war crimes. Nor will the Provisionals or the other republican factions guilty of killing civilians be immune from the charge either. To take just one example — under the rules of war such as the Geneva Convention prisoners of war have fundamental rights on capture and should not according to those international principles be killed while in captivity. Is it too outlandish then to argue that the very public 'arrest', beating, torture and execution of the two British corporals in west Belfast at an IRA funeral in 1988 was tantamount to a war crime? Could it be possible that under the guise of the conflict being a war, the relatives or loved ones of those executed POWs will rush to the International Court of Justice in The Hague and ask for those at leadership level within the IRA to be put on trial? In all three cases it could potentially be the leaders of states and paramilitary organisations and their political front organisations that may face trial in the future. And that is probably one of the reasons why that particular Bradley-Eames proposal will never be accepted.

The Provisional IRA killed more people than any of the other main actors in the tragedy of the Northern Troubles. Their final casualty, however, has been the truth. So much so that in February 2008 they announced that they would not be co-operating with the Bradley-Eames process in examining the recent past. They accused the Consultative Group on the Past of being drawn up by the British and thus somehow compromised. It was a telling decision. For one, Eames and Bradley had uncovered a staggering amount of information from sources such as the Stevens Inquiry pointing to the extent to which the British state had infiltrated and directed all paramilitary organisations. This included the IRA and in one instance the two unofficial truth commissioners had been shown three filing cabinets by the Stevens team containing documents pertaining to the running of informers inside the PIRA. For an organisation that has expended so much energy trying to rewrite history it was hardly ever likely it would willingly hand over the power to change and distort the past to an agency it could not control or manipulate.

Northern Ireland meanwhile has ended up being run by the twin destructive forces of Provoism and Paisleyism, the two movements that for four decades frustrated so many political initiatives and cut short the careers of a long line of leaders prepared for compromise. But as they licked their wounds after the 2007 electoral mauling in the Republic at the 2008 Ard Fheis and prepared for the latest Easter Rising commemorations, Sinn Féin suddenly found themselves facing a new political partner in the North. On 4 March 2008 Ian Paisley announced he was to retire, his final curtain call being the May International Investment Conference in Belfast hosted by Bill Clinton. Paisley's departure signalled the end of the 'Chuckle Brothers' experience.

The unlikely duo were to have a couple of final shows together before the Big Man bowed out and the first came just twenty-four hours after Paisley revealed he was heading for retirement. The setting was Victoria Square in central Belfast, a gleaming dome-topped new cathedral of commerce that has attracted big UK retail chains such as the House of Fraser. Paisley and McGuinness were invited to officially open the new centre under the helpful eye and prompting of TV star Eamon Holmes. Baroness Eileen Paisley turned up alongside her son Ian Junior, the subject of so much controversy over links to builders and businessmen throughout the first year of the post St Andrews mandatory coalition government.

Suspended above the stage where Paisley and McGuinness sat were a series of flat-screen televisions, which broadcast a film involving a grandfather telling a child about the history of Belfast. The shortest of the historic sequences, which went from the construction of the *Titanic* to the two world wars and beyond into the future, was a series of images from the Troubles. There were, however, no pictures of shopping centres being blown up or gun battles or riots. The Troubles were represented on screen by snapshots of various loyalist and republican murals that are still on walls in west and north Belfast. History, even at thirty frames a second, was being re-edited and glossed over, the recent past presented as a row of tourist-trap images.

Martin McGuinness in his speech had warm, generous praise for Paisley and his wife Eileen. He wished the First Minister all the very best for the future and hoped he and his wife could enjoy their retirement.

Following the spectacular displays of acrobatics with men and women descending from the roof of the dome on ropes, in a scene reminiscent of a James Bond movie where the good guys — thanks to 007 — break into the super-villain's lair, McGuinness had to leave and face more mundane matters back up in the Assembly.

The next morning McGuinness was scheduled to meet with Peter Robinson, Paisley's then deputy in the DUP, and seek to hammer out a compromise over a bid by Sinn Féin to commemorate IRA woman Mairéad Farrell. Sinn Féin MLA's had planned to hold a memorial service to the IRA member, who was shot dead in Gibraltar by the SAS, inside Stormont's ornate Long Gallery. Unionists objected and the event instead was shifted to Sinn Féin's party room inside the parliament buildings.

The row over the Farrell commemoration merely reflected the frostiness behind all the smiles of the 'Chuckle Brothers'; it demonstrated that there was little common ground beyond a collective yearning to cling to devolved power by the two parties. At the time of writing, Peter Robinson is about to be elevated to the post of First Minister. He and his party have made clear they will have a very different relationship with the Deputy First Minister, one that will be bloodless, business-like and technocratic.

Robinson is, like his predecessor, a unionist politician who has provoked hatred and ire among Northern Ireland nationalists down through the decades. His hard-line rhetoric and short-tempered outbursts on television throughout the Troubles frightened and repelled generations of nationalists and republicans. He and his followers' 'invasion' of Clontibret in County Monaghan in 1986 ended with him going to jail in the Irish Republic. He was later attacked with stones and Molotov cocktails during a court appearance in Dundalk connected to the border incursion.

From the viewpoint of purist republicanism, the outcome post May 2008 is perhaps even worse than the spectacle of McGuinness smiling and joking at Paisley's side. Sinn Féin has now been robbed even of the smiles and the laughter. Mainstream republicans have played a major role in delivering Peter Robinson as First Minister of Northern Ireland. Barring physical illness or accident Robinson will hold the highest office in the Assembly until 2011, the year of the next round of elections to Stormont. The DUP then plan, if they remain the largest party, a seamless hand-over of power to Nigel Dodds, their North Belfast MP. That will be just four short years before the 100th anniversary of the Easter Rising.

Postscript

The Fallacy of the 'Good Example'

It was arguably the most unlikely of places to illuminate the chasm between Irish republican and Islamist terrorism. The 'Star Letter' of the January 2008 edition of the British toilet humour magazine/comic *Viz* counter-posed the terrorism of the IRA and Al Qaeda. The correspondent, one Nick Pettigrew from London, wrote:

'Thirty years ago, the Irish were our most feared terrorists and now they have theme pubs everywhere. So by 2047 will Britain be full of Islamic Extremist theme pubs? Because I don't much like the sound of that.'

On a frivolous level the joke is a cheap jibe at the Irish, all the Irish, including all of those Irish, the majority on the island and beyond, who detested the 'armed struggle'. But on another plane the quip actually exposes the radical difference between republican paramilitaries and the soldiers of extreme Islam. Because it suggests that despite all the ruthlessness, dedication to cause and self-sacrifice, Irish republicans have always had other, more worldly concerns.

Their universe was not completely consumed by an all-encompassing theology even if at times republicans behaved fanatically and acted as if on some messianic mission. The contrast is worth exploring because since the peace process, the ceasefires and the present historic compromise at Stormont, it has become fashionable to hold up the North of Ireland as a good example for other conflicts, as a template to bring all those other interminable struggles across the planet to an end.

At present it has become vogue in certain British Foreign Office circles, among former members of MI6, pro-Arab sections of academia and the liberal press to draw comfort from the example of the Irish peace process. In particular a number of influential voices in British public life have been arguing that once upon a time it was taboo to talk to the IRA. However, secret channels set up between the Provos and British Intelligence (and hence Her Majesty's government) eventually bore fruit with the 1994 ceasefires and all the changes that flowed from it. Hence, these voices contend, if only the West could do the same with Islamist movements such as Hamas and Hezbollah in the Middle East and even some sections of the Taliban in Afghanistan there could be room for optimism, even an end to these conflicts.

On the surface this thesis appears seductive: if the most sophisticated terrorist organisation in the Western world can be brought in from the cold then surely the same can be done with the likes of Hamas and Hezbollah.

However, the formula is in fact entirely bogus and anti-historical.

The parallels between the Irish republican death cult and the Islamist one appears at first to be remarkably similar.

Groups like the IRA, Hamas and Hezbollah seem to revel in the iconography of martyrdom. One of the most striking things I noticed on a first visit to the Shia heartlands of South Lebanon was the profusion of posters of fallen fighters and murals depicting their new status in a rainbowed paradise after-life of flowing fountains and doves along the walls of towns and villages where Hezbollah and the more openly pro-Syrian Amal were dominant. The iconic imagery, in terms of both tone and style, is almost exactly like those murals of the Irish hunger strikers and fallen IRA 'volunteers' that, prior to the latter stages of the peace process, covered the walls of west Belfast and Derry, even down to the ubiquitous beards. Moreover, the willingness of IRA and INLA prisoners to sacrifice themselves on hunger strike, to starve themselves to death in pursuit of political causes, seemed to equate with the self-immolaters who strap bombs to their bodies, killing themselves as well as their enemies. But in fact this is where the comparisons end and the contrasts begin.

Irish republicans throughout the generations have never lacked physical courage in pursuit of their goals. They have, however, been subject to certain boundaries imposed by their own particular background and culture. Throughout the hunger strike the prisoners' supporters insisted that their fast for political status was not long-drawn-out suicide, which for centuries was regarded as a sin in Catholic theology. It seems puzzling none the less that a political movement that produced activists willing to starve themselves to death for a cause would regard suicide bombing as anathema.

Tommy Gorman, as head of the IRA's 'Engineering Department' in the Belfast in the 1980s, knew many young men and women willing to transport bombs into the city centre and to security bases. They risked death or arrest as couriers of lethal explosive devices. Yet Gorman recalls that during the armed campaign no one ever volunteered for a suicide mission against a British army or RUC target.

The IRA veteran who literally swam into republican folklore in 1972 when he escaped from the *Maidstone* prison ship moored in Belfast Lough is best positioned to explain why no one was willing to destroy themselves along with others in a few seconds for the 'struggle'.

'In all the years I was in the IRA there wasn't a single volunteer I came across who came forward willing to be a suicide-bomber. The hunger strike was different because for the prisoners there was always a back-door to life. At any time their demands could have been met and the fast would have been over and their lives saved. That's the crucial difference.'

Gorman is visibly amused at the notion that there would have been a reservoir of suicide-bombers: 'Even if anybody had come forward with the idea that they wanted to blow themselves up alongside Brits or cops he would have been sent packing. He wouldn't have been taken seriously.'

It is telling that the closest PIRA came to Islamic-style suicide bombing was to use proxies, those forced at gunpoint to become 'human bombs'. It is also revealing that the tactic was quickly abandoned by the Provisionals following a wave of national revulsion against such an inhuman strategy.

On 24 October 1990 PIRA launched a series of co-ordinated 'human bomb' attacks on four separate British army vehicle checkpoints across Northern Ireland. The largest loss of life occurred at the Coshquin checkpoint on the Derry-Donegal border. The 'human bomb' chosen for the attack was Patsy Gillespie, a Catholic civilian who worked in the canteen of a local British army base and was thus regarded by republicans as a 'collaborator'. Patsy Gillespie was forced at gunpoint into a van packed with 1,000 lbs of explosives. He was strapped into the driver's seat and ordered to drive at top speed into the checkpoint. Gillespie had been told his wife was being held by an armed gang at their home in the nationalist Shantallow area. As soon as he arrived at the checkpoint the IRA detonated the bomb inside the van by remote control, blowing Patsy Gillespie and five British soldiers apart. On the same day the IRA in South Armagh tried the same tactic by strapping a local South Armagh man into a van loaded with explosives. On this occasion the driver managed to dive out of the vehicle before impact. One soldier died at the checkpoint near Newry. A third attack using a 'human bomb' was foiled outside Roslea, Co. Fermanagh.

Ed Moloney in his masterpiece *A Secret History of the IRA* has described the 'human bomb' tactic as a public relations disaster for the Provisionals. The almost instant abandonment of this ultra-cynical, callous means of delivering huge bombs to British bases is further proof of the limits Irish politics and culture placed upon the 'armed struggle'. In Gaza, from the destruction of the Twin Towers on 9/11 to the resumption of suicide bombs in Israel on 4 February 2008, Palestinians openly celebrated the exploits of suicide murderers in the streets; in Ireland the use of the 'human bombs' sickened an entire nation and drove the mass of the Irish people even further away from the Provisionals' project. Moreover, as Moloney has argued with some justification, national revulsion against the 'human bomb' murders eventually reinforced that faction of the republican movement determined to run down and ultimately end the armed campaign. The cult of Irish republicanism may be rooted in blood sacrifice but when it came to the 'human bombs' it was the blood sacrifice of others.

It is not just the contrasting tactics that radically differentiate the pragmatic Provisionals with the theocratic militants of Hamas and Hezbollah. Throughout their campaign of terror the Provisionals always sought out an 'address' to deliver offers of negotiation. It was, of course, generally speaking to the wrong one — the British government, rather than the true 'British presence', i.e. the unionists. None the less from the very outset the Provisionals were eager to open up dialogue with their enemies. Indeed there is anecdotal evidence that in the 1990s a modus operandi was established between the UVF and PIRA in Belfast to avoid the two organisations 'taking out' each other's respective leaderships. In some cases senior IRA figures in the city alongside their old rivals in the Officials also met with loyalists on a regular basis to carve up building site rackets in the city, particularly in the 1980s.

Islamist movements have no 'address' because they don't recognise its right to exist, namely Israel. Rather they seek its ultimate destruction. In the end the Provisionals have had to settle for something far less than their ultimate goal of a United Ireland. Movements such as Hamas are maximalist by nature, they are all-or-nothing organisations which regard any compromise as tantamount to or even worse than religious apostasy. That is why throughout the period of the Oslo peace process in the mid-1990s, Hamas and its offshoots and allies resorted to the tactic of blowing up buses, cafés and bars in Israel proper as a means of destroying the accord between the Labour dominated government in Jerusalem and the more secular Fatah under Yasser Arafat. Unlike Irish republicans the entire Islamist worldview is coloured by an unbending theology rooted in the early centuries of the last Millennium; republicanism, at least in theory, as opposed to the Provos' malpractice of it, is rooted in the eighteenth-century European Enlightenment.

The narrative of the Irish peace process suggests a leadership driven by entirely practical concerns, willing when necessary to dump old ideological certainties in the pursuit of limited goals. Dissidents jibe that Sinn Féin's entry into and embrace of the parliament at Stormont would be akin in the Middle East to Hamas entering the Knesset. In that at least the dissidents have a point.

But even the most militant dissident Irish republican, while admiring of Hamas and Hezbollah's obduracy, has not resorted to one of their principal tactics — suicide murders. In the period before, during and after the Good Friday Agreement was signed there were plenty of bombs detonated aimed at undermining support for Trimbleite unionism in the same way as Hamas and Islamic Jihad tried (and were arguably successful) to erode Israeli public support for the Oslo peace process. However, even after the Real IRA caused such carnage at Omagh the dissidents immediately stepped back from the brink and declared their own cessations of violence. In addition the Real IRA didn't deliberately set out to kill civilians including women and children. Their operatives botched the placing of the car bomb in the town centre and failed to give an adequate warning. Clearly the

Real IRA, just as the Provisionals had done before them, recklessly put civilians at risk in their bid to kill members of the security forces and cause massive economic damage. But there is a distinct difference between the Irish republican dissidents' lethal carelessness and the deliberate targeting of pizza parlours, discos and even Irish bars in Tel Aviv and Jerusalem where the operative (the suicide-murderer) knows he is going to kill men, women and children.

Leaving aside the absence of the suicide-bomb in the Real IRA and Continuity IRA's arsenals, both organisations could, if they only got lucky once, detonate bombs that could in an instant shake the political institutions up at Stormont to their foundations. They could mimic that other barbaric strategy of the Sunni Jihadists and ex-Baathists in Iraq who have bombed Shia mosques and districts in order to foment outright sectarian civil war. RIRA, CIRA and any other faction to emerge in the near future could follow suit and indiscriminately bomb Protestant heartlands. But they chose not to do so partly to pay lip service to Wolfe Tone's original definition of Irish republicanism and in the main because they know deep down the disaster they would be bringing down not only on themselves but also the community from which they come. The parallels therefore between the rejectionist republicans and the Islamic militants of all hues, Shia and Sunni, are entirely illusory.

Given the frequent exposures of informers, agents and spies inside the Provisionals it has become blindingly obvious that the British had a deep insight into the direction that sections of the IRA leadership, most critically its Belfast-based commanders, wished the organisation to travel. They encouraged, persuaded and, if Brian Nelson, the British army's spy inside the UDA, is correct, also ensured certain republican leaders like Gerry Adams stayed where they were in the long-term interests of a peaceful settlement. By contrast, no single figure like Adams appears to be emerging, or is likely to emerge, from inside Hamas that can tilt the Islamist movement away from its all-or-nothing ideology.

The fallacy of the 'good example', even applies to less extreme conflicts such as the struggle between the Spanish state and the Basque terrorists of ETA. Although ETA's 'war' has lasted longer than the Provisional IRA's, it has not only claimed fewer lives (under 900 victims), the Basque separatist organisation has undergone almost double the number of splits and schisms than republicanism over the last forty years. There have been aborted attempts to push ETA and Madrid towards negotiations, which have involved the likes of Fr Alec Reid, one of the two Clonard priests that played such a critical role in helping Adams reverse the Provisionals out of the armed struggle cul de sac. Once again, however, there is a crucial difference in the quality of leadership. So far the present ETA leadership has proved as intractable and ideologically rigid as those in charge of Republican Sinn Féin or those allied to the Real IRA. If ETA and its political wing followed mainstream Sinn Féin's example then they would have to settle for what has already been on offer since the 1978 post-Franco constitution: devolved autonomy but within the Spanish state. This is essentially what the Good Friday Agreement and later the deal at St Andrews resulted in for Northern Ireland. So for ETA to accept its equivalent on the Iberian Peninsula would be tantamount to total surrender. Given the nihilism of ETA's seemingly endless violent campaign as witnessed in the cold-blooded murder of a former Spanish Socialist Party member in the Basque region just prior to the 2008 General Election, there appears to be no evidence that realism is dawning among the Etarras (militants). As we approach the end of the first decade of the twenty-first century it appears that ETA still have evidently learned nothing from the Irish peace process.

One of the process's mini-growth industries over the last decade has been the travelling caravan of ex-paramilitaries, both loyalist and republican, alongside politicians who have visited almost every other conflict zone on the planet since the ceasefires were declared. They have journeyed from Israel/Palestine to South Africa, from Latin America to Sri Lanka. In each unresolved region of discord the local warring parties have sought out advice and succour from some of the key protagonists of Ireland's 'war'. Former enemies such as the late David Ervine and Martin McGuinness have travelled both to the disputed Jaffa peninsula and to Israel-Palestine where they relayed their experiences on how to shut down conflict and de-activate underground armies. They went there no doubt because they genuinely believed they could do some good. Perhaps they might succeed somehow.

In arguably the most dangerous of any of those conflict zones, Iraq, the advice of another major actor in Northern Ireland has been sought out — the British government and its security forces. Representatives of the Iraqi government in 2007 were fascinated to learn from PSNI officers training and liaising with local police in Basra and Baghdad that the British state had constructed and paid for a crude mechanism to dramatically reduce sectarian slaughter — the building of the gloriously misnamed 'peace walls' separating

Protestant and Catholic areas, particularly in Belfast. PSNI officers returning from Iraq later remarked that the Iraqi authorities were embarking on a series of similar walled barriers which would 'protect' rival Sunni and Shia areas from one another.

The other 'authorities' in Iraq, namely the Americans, also realised they had something to learn from how Britain slowly but surely defeated the 'armed struggle'. As Mary Ann Clancy pointed out in her survey of the Bush Administration's attitude to Northern Ireland, the Americans were fascinated by Britain's secret war against the IRA. Those US State Department and White House officials who spoke to Clancy appeared far more interested in Britain's use of informants inside the IRA, and externally the promotion of potential peace faction, within the republican movement, than in the nurturing of all-encompassing political dialogue between the warring parties. The only 'good example' the Americans saw from the Northern Ireland conflict was the one that Britain used to close down the IRA's armed campaign. The Americans at least had seen through the smoke and mirrors of the Irish peace process and the polite fiction that the final outcome had been some sort of honourable draw.

ANYONE CAN GLORY IN A
TRIUMPH BUT
IT TAKES REAL TALENT
TO PORTRAY DEFEAT
AS A
VICTORY, NOT?

Index